Building Fluency: Lessons and Strategies for Reading Success

by Wiley Blevins

SCHOLASTIC
PROFESSIONAL BOOKS

New York • Toronto • London • Auckland • Sydney
Mexico City • New Delhi • Hong Kong • Buenos Aires

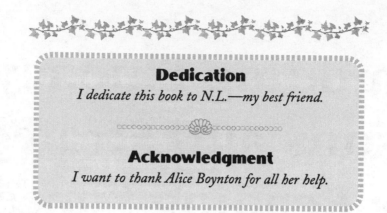

Dedication

I dedicate this book to N.L.—my best friend.

Acknowledgment

I want to thank Alice Boynton for all her help.

Edited by Jeanette Moss

Cover design by Kenneth Powell

Interior design by Sydney Wright

Cover photo by Bruce Cramer

Interior Photo Credits:
Page 4: Dynamic Graphics; Page 13: Digital Stock; Title page and pages 9, 14, and 25: PhotoDisk;
Page 17: Richard Hutchings; Page 19: Ken O'Donoghue

ISBN 0–439–28838–X

Contents

Section 1

What Is Reading Fluency?

R ecently, *after several amazing trips to Israel, I began studying Hebrew. Since Hebrew doesn't employ the English alphabet, I was forced to learn a whole new set of symbols and sound-spelling correspondences. At first these strange-looking squiggles and lines*

Building Fluency Scholastic Professional Books

were meaningless to me. I tried everything I use with my students to learn them as quickly as possible. I wrote each letter as I said its sound. I created a set of flash cards and went over the cards several times a day. I even found a computer program that focused on learning the letters and contained mastery tests. After a couple weeks I felt ready to tackle my first simple Hebrew text. As I began to read, I struggled through every word, searched my mind for each letter-sound, blended the sounds together, then tried to recall the meaning of the word I had pronounced. Often, by the time I worked my way to the end of a sentence, I had forgotten what was at the beginning. My slow, labored, and inefficient reading was (and still is, unfortunately) characteristic of one who has not acquired reading fluency.

The Tale of Five Balloons by Miriam Roth

Fluency: A Definition

According to *A Dictionary of Reading and Related Terms* (Harris and Hodges, 1981), fluency is "the ability to read smoothly, easily, and readily with freedom from word recognition problems." Fluency is necessary for good comprehension and enjoyable reading (Nathan and Stanovich, 1991). A lack of fluency is characterized by a slow, halting pace; frequent mistakes; poor phrasing; and inadequate intonation (Samuels, 1979)—all the result of weak word recognition skills.

Fluent reading is a major goal of reading instruction because decoding print accurately and effortlessly enables students to read for meaning. Students who decode words effortlessly can focus more of their conscious attention to making meaning from text. For many students, fluency begins around grades 2 to 3, in Stage 2 of reading development, the "Confirmation, Fluency, and Ungluing from Print" stage. (See Chall's Six Stages of Reading Development on page 6.) During this fluency stage, readers become "unglued" from the print; that is, students can recognize many words quickly and accurately by sight and are skilled at sounding out those they don't recognize by sight. A fluent reader can:

1. read at a rapid rate (pace—the speed at which oral or silent reading occurs)

2. automatically recognize words (smoothness/accuracy—efficient decoding skills)

3. phrase correctly (prosody—the ability to read a text orally using appropriate pitch, stress, and phrasing).

The Six Stages of Reading Development

The stages of reading development, proposed by Chall (1983), provides a clear and useful framework for how children learn to read. This framework includes six reading levels.

Stage 0: Birth Through Age Six

Prereading: The most notable change during this stage is the child's growing control over language. By the time a child enters grade one (at around age six), he or she has approximately 6,000 words in his or her listening and speaking vocabularies. During this stage, children also develop some knowledge of print, such as recognizing a few letters, words, and environmental print signs. Many children are able to write their names. It is common to see these children "pretend read" a book that has been repeatedly read to them. At this stage, children "bring more to the printed page than they take out."

Stage 1: Grades 1 Through 2

Initial Reading or Decoding: During this time, children develop an understanding of the alphabetic principle and begin to use their knowledge of sound-spelling relationships to decode words.

Stage 2: Grades 2 Through 3

Confirmation, Fluency, and Ungluing from Print: During this stage, children further develop and solidify their decoding skills. They also develop additional strategies to decode words and make meaning from text. As this stage ends, children have developed fluency; that is, they can recognize many words quickly and accurately by sight and are skilled at sounding out words they don't recognize by sight. They are also skilled at using context clues.

Stage 3: Grades 4 Through 8

Learning the New: During this stage, reading demands change. Children begin to use reading more as a way to obtain information and learn about the values, attitudes, and insights of others. Texts contain many words not already in a child's speaking and listening vocabularies. These texts, frequently drawn from a wide variety of genres, also extend beyond the background experiences of the children.

Stage 4: Throughout High School (Grades 9 Through 12)

Multiple Viewpoints: During this stage, readers encounter more complex language and vocabulary as they read texts in more advanced content areas. Thus the language and cognitive demands required of the reader increase. Readers are also reading texts containing varying viewpoints and are required to analyze them critically.

Stage 5: Throughout College and Beyond

Construction and Reconstruction: This stage is characterized by a "world view." Readers use the information in books and articles as needed; that is, a reader knows which books and articles will provide the information he or she needs and can locate that information within a book without having to read it in its entirety. At this stage, reading is considered constructive; that is, readers take in a wide range of information and construct their own understanding for their individual uses based on their analysis and synthesis of the information. Not all readers progress to this stage.

—J.S. Chall. *Stages of Reading Development.* McGraw-Hill. 1983

Building Fluency Scholastic Professional Books

Nonfluent readers read slowly and spend so much time trying to identify unfamiliar words that they have trouble comprehending what they're reading.

Automaticity theory, developed by LaBerge and Samuels (1974), helps explain how reading fluency develops. Automaticity refers to knowing how to do something so well you don't have to think about it. As tasks become easier, they require less attention and practice. Think of a child learning to play basketball. As initial attention is focused on how to dribble the ball, it's difficult for the child to think about guarding the ball from opponents, shooting a basket, or even running quickly down the court. However, over time, lots of practice makes dribbling almost second nature. The player is ready to concentrate on higher-level aspects of the game.

For reading, automaticity refers to the ability to accurately and quickly recognize many words as whole units. The advantage of recognizing a word as a whole unit is that words have meaning, and less memory is required for a meaningful word than for a meaningless letter. The average child needs between 4 and 14 exposures to a new word to recognize it automatically. However, children with reading difficulties need 40 or more exposures to a new word. Therefore, it's critical that students get a great deal of practice reading stories at their independent reading level to develop automaticity (Beck & Juel, 1995; Samuels, Schermer, and Reinking, 1992).

To commit words to memory, children need to decode many words sound by sound, and then progress to recognizing the larger word chunks. Now, instead of focusing on sounding out words sound by sound, the reader can read whole words, thereby focusing attention on decoding and comprehension simultaneously. In fact, the hallmark of fluent reading is the ability to decode and comprehend at the same time.

Although research has shown that fluency is a critical factor in reading development, many teachers and publishers have failed to recognize its importance to overall reading proficiency. Few teachers teach fluency directly, and elementary reading textbooks give fluency instruction short shrift. Consequently, Allington (1983) has called fluency the "neglected goal" of reading instruction.

There are many reasons why children fail to read fluently. Allington (1983) cites the following:

* *Lack of exposure.* Some children have never been exposed to fluent reading models. These children come from homes in which there are few books and little or no reading.

* *The good-reader syndrome.* In school, good readers are more likely to get positive feedback and are more likely to be encouraged to read with expression and make meaning from text.

Poor readers receive less positive feedback, and the focus of their instruction is often solely on figuring out words or attending to word parts.

* **Lack of practice time.** Good readers generally spend more time reading during instructional time and therefore become better readers. Good readers also engage in more silent reading. This additional practice stimulates their reading growth. Poor readers spend less time actually reading.

* **Frustration.** Good readers are exposed to more text at their independent reading level, whereas poor readers frequently encounter text at their frustration level. Consequently, poor readers tend to give up because they make so many errors.

* **Missing the "why" of reading.** Good readers tend to view reading as making meaning from text, whereas poor readers tend to view reading as trying to read words accurately.

Put It Into Practice!

Evaluating Slow Readers

To find out why a student is reading slowly, ask her to read a passage from a book below her reading level. If she reads the passage slowly, her problem is probably poor fluency. If she can read the text easily, she's probably having trouble with decoding or comprehension. Here are two ways to determine whether the student's problem is with decoding or comprehension:

1. Have the student read an on-level passage and then ask a series of questions. If she accurately answers 75% or more of the questions, then the problem is one of weak decoding skills. To help this student with her decoding skills, have her read from material at a lower level, involve her in repeated reading or echo readings in which the student echoes phrases or sentences read by the teacher (see page 41), and have her practice read dictated stories that she created and you recorded on chart paper.

2. Give the student a running list of the words he will encounter in a text. If he can't recognize 95% of the words, then decoding is likely the issue. If he does recognize 95% or more of the words but has difficulty reading, then comprehension or fluency is the issue. A major reason students experience reading difficulty is that too much is taught too fast. Go back to where they are successful and start again.

Assessing Reading Fluency

*I*n order to help students develop fluency, you must first know their oral reading accuracy and rate. There are several measurement tools you can use to identify the accuracy and rate, and nationally-normed averages exist. Many state standards now include these rates as benchmarks of students' reading progress.

The combination of reading accuracy and rate is referred to as a student's oral reading fluency (ORF). It is expressed as "words correct per minute" (WCPM).

It is essential to measure both accuracy and rate. For example, if you measure only accuracy, you won't know that it takes one student twice as long to read the same text as it does another student. Which student is fluent? Likewise, if you measure only rate, you wouldn't know that one student, who could read a text much more quickly than another student, makes significantly more mistakes. Which student is fluent?

Words Per Minute—The Key to Reading Progress

The number of words read correctly per minute is an important indicator of a student's progress in all aspects of reading—decoding, fluency, and comprehension. Twenty years of research by Germann (Edformation, 2001) has shown strong correlations between standardized achievement test scores and the number of words read correctly per minute (WCPM).

Standardized Reading Test	Words Read Correctly Per Minute Correlation
Stanford Diagnostic Reading Test	.94
Woodcock Reading Mastery Test (Word Identification)	.94
SAT Comprehension	.91
Woodcock Reading Mastery Test (Comprehension)	.84

Oral-Reading Fluency and Standardized Reading Test Correlations

Using the procedure detailed in "Measuring Reading Rate" along with the "Oral Reading Fluency Norms" charts on page 11, you can zero in on your students' reading fluency levels. Here are some guidelines for scoring the Oral Fluency measurement:

Measuring Reading Rate

To determine a student's oral reading rate, take a one-minute, timed sampling of his or her oral reading of a passage at his reading level. The passage must be unfamiliar to the student, can be taken from any grade-level textbook or book series, and must contain a minimum of 200 words. Make a copy of the passage for the student and one for yourself, so you can record any errors while he or she reads. As the student reads, follow along and mark on your copy any words incorrectly read. Use the guidelines that follow. For example, if a student stops or struggles with a word for 3 seconds, say the word and mark it as incorrect. Place a mark after the last word read. Then, tally the results and consult the "Oral Reading Fluency Norms" charts for Grades 2–5 and 6–8 on page 11. Using these norms, you can determine how your students rate nationally and which students need more work in developing fluency.

Note: Some educators suggest using three passages to avoid the content of any one passage affecting the fluency score. Have the student read each passage for one minute, noting all three scores. The median (middle) score is the student's fluency score for that testing period. For example, if a student scores 100, 102, and 110, his fluency score is 102. Use the same three passages for testing in the fall, winter, and spring.

Building Fluency   Scholastic Professional Books

Words read correctly. These are words that the student pronounces correctly, given the reading context.

* Count self-corrections within 3 seconds as correct.

* Don't count repetitions as incorrect.

Words read incorrectly. Count the following types of errors as incorrect: (a) mispronunciations, (b) substitutions, and (c) omissions. Also, count words the student doesn't read within 3 seconds as incorrect.

* Mispronunciations are words that are misread: *bell* for *ball*.

* Substitutions are words that are substituted for the correct word; this is often inferred by a one-to-one correspondence between word orders: *dog* for *cat*.

* Omissions are words skipped or not read; if a student skips an entire line, each word is counted as an error.

3-second rule. If a student is struggling to pronounce a word or hesitates for 3 seconds, tell the student the word, and count it as an error.

Oral Reading Fluency Norms, Grades 2–5
(J.E. Hansbrouck and G. Tindal, 1992)

Grade	Percentile	WCPM* Fall	WCPM Winter	WCPM Spring
2	75%	82	106	124
	50%	53	78	94
	25%	23	46	65
3	75%	107	123	142
	50%	79	93	114
	25%	65	70	87
4	75%	125	133	143
	50%	99	112	118
	25%	72	89	92
5	75%	126	143	151
	50%	105	118	128
	25%	77	93	100

*WCPM = words correct per minute

Oral Reading Fluency Norms, Grades 6–8
(G. Germann, 2001)

Grade	Percentile	WCPM* Fall	WCPM Winter	WCPM Spring
6	90%	171	184	200
	75%	143	161	172
	50%	115	133	145
	25%	91	106	116
	10%	71	82	91
7	90%	200	206	212
	75%	174	182	193
	50%	148	158	167
	25%	124	133	145
	10%	104	115	124
8	90%	206	217	223
	75%	183	193	198
	50%	155	165	171
	25%	128	141	146
	10%	101	112	118

*WCPM = words correct per minute**

**Current Oral Reading Fluency Norms for Grades 1–8 can be found at: www.edformation.com. Note: Oral Reading Fluency (ORF) norms are updated in the fall, winter, and spring of each school year. They are from an electronic aggregation of all students using Edformation's AIMSweb Benchmark Web-based software and Edformation's Standard Oral Reading Benchmark Passages. Questions can be directed to Edformation, Inc., 6420 Flying Cloud Drive, Suite 204, Eden Prairie, MN 55344. Call 952-944-1882 or fax 952-944-1884.

How to Interpret and Use the Fluency Norms

The norms are listed as percentile scores. For example, a percentile score of 65 means that 65% of students received fluency scores equal to or lower than the number indicated. Generally, students reading at the 50th percentile will have good comprehension of grade-level texts. Therefore, a fourth-grade student reading at 118 WCPM (50th percentile) would be expected to have at least adequate comprehension of grade-level text at the end of the year. A fourth grader who reads 143 WCPM (75th percentile) would be expected to have excellent comprehension of grade-level text at the end of the year. Those reading at 92 WCPM (25th percentile) would, however, be expected to have difficulty comprehending grade-level text.

You can use these norms to make classroom decisions (Hansbrouck and Tindal, 1992).

* Screening and determining student eligibility for intervention programs
* Setting instructional goals and objectives
* Placing students in instructional groups
* Selecting appropriate reading materials for students
* Monitoring academic progress of students
* Reporting student progress to parents
* Making adjustments to, or changes in, reading instruction

Building Fluency Scholastic Professional Books

Section 3

Six Ways to Develop Fluency

*A*lthough few reading-textbook teacher manuals contain instruction on building fluency, there are in fact many things you can do to develop your students' fluency. Rasinski (1994) has identified six ways to build fluency.

1. Model fluent reading

Students need many opportunities to hear texts read. This can include daily teacher read-alouds, books on tape, and books read by peers during book-sharing time. It's particularly critical for poorer readers who've been placed in a low reading group to hear text read correctly because they are likely to repeatedly hear the efforts of other poor readers in their group. They need proficient, fluent models; that is, they need to have a model voice in their heads to refer to as they monitor their own reading. While you read aloud to students, periodically highlight aspects of fluent reading. For example, point out how you read dialogue the way you think the character might have said it or how you speed up your reading when the text becomes more intense and exciting. Talk about fluency—how to achieve it, and why it's important. Continually remind students that with practice they can become fluent readers. Another important benefit of daily read-alouds is that they expose students to a wider range of vocabulary.

Teacher Talk

"Listen to me read this paragraph. Note how I read each sentence as if I'm saying it to a friend. The last sentence ends in an exclamation mark. Listen to the way I raise my voice to show excitement!"

"A strong reader reads at a good speed and can pronounce all of the words correctly. Becoming strong readers will be one of our goals this year. You may need to read a story many times to read it correctly and at a good pace. Rereading a story can also be a lot of fun."

"Listen to how I read this sentence. Read it after me in the same way. When you read, think about how I sounded. Did I pause after any words? Did I raise or lower my voice?"

2. Provide direct instruction and feedback

Direct instruction and feedback in fluency includes, but isn't limited to, independent reading practice, fluent reading modeling, and monitoring students' reading rates. Here are some ways to include lots of this needed instruction in your classroom.

* ***Explicitly teach students the sound-spelling correspondences they struggle with, high-utility decoding and syllabication strategies, and a large core of sight words.*** Use the phonics and sight-word assessments on pages 73–74 to determine each student's skill needs.

Building Fluency Scholastic Professional Books

* **Have students practice reading new or difficult words prior to reading a text.** Scan a text before you introduce it and select 15–20 words that you think may cause your students difficulty. Help students decode each word using phonics and syllabication strategies. Then, have them practice reading the list chorally several times before reading the story.

* **Time students' reading occasionally.** Have them create charts to monitor their own progress. Encourage them to set new reading-rate goals. (See reproducible chart, page 16.)

* **Include oral recitation lessons.** (Hoffman, 1987; Hoffman and Crone, 1985). With this technique the focus is on comprehension. Introduce a story and read it aloud. Discuss the content with the class and have the class create a story summary. Then discuss the prosodic (phrasing and intonation) elements of the text (e.g., reading dialogue as if it is spoken; reading all caps louder; differentiating between question and statement voices; understanding a character's expressed emotion—anger, sadness, joy, or disgust; and reading longer phrases with appropriate pauses). Then have students practice reading sections of the story both on their own and with your guidance. Finally, have individual students read sections of the story aloud for the class. Monitor each student's reading rate and word-recognition accuracy.

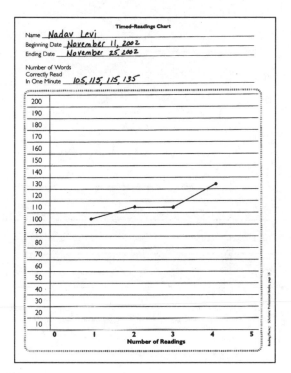

* **Teach students about "smooshing" the words together.** Some poor readers mistakenly believe that they are supposed to read each word separately, consequently they always sound like they are reading a list. Model fluent reading by reading a passage without pauses between words. Then read the passage using appropriate pauses and phrasing. Discuss the differences.

* **Explain the return-sweep eye movement.** For some students, return sweeps are difficult. As a result, they lose their place as they read. A common technique to overcome this is to place a sheet of paper or a bookmark under the line as one reads and move it down line by line. For many students this is disruptive because it halts the natural return-sweep motion. So some reading specialists suggest placing the bookmark above the line to avoid interfering with the return sweep.

To illustrate for students how our eyes move as we read, poke a pencil-sized hole in a sheet of paper and hold it twelve inches away as you read a passage. Have the students comment on the jerkiness of your eyes (and your reading) as you move from word to word and line to line. This observation can result in an "aha moment" for some students.

Timed-Readings Chart

Name _____

Beginning Date _____

Ending Date _____

Number of Words
Correctly Read
in One Minute _____

200						
190						
180						
170						
160						
150						
140						
130						
120						
110						
100						
90						
80						
70						
60						
50						
40						
30						
20						
10						
	0	1	2	3	4	5

Number of Readings

* **Teach students about the eye-voice span.** When we read aloud, there is a distinct and measurable distance between our eye placement and our voice. Our eyes are one to three words ahead of our oral reading. To illustrate this phenomenon, copy a story or passage onto a transparency. As you are about to finish a paragraph, turn off the transparency. Students will be amazed that you can still say a few words. They'll see how fluent readers phrase chunks appropriately.

* **Find alternatives to round-robin reading.** Round-robin reading is one of the most harmful techniques for developing fluency. During round-robin reading, students read aloud only a small portion of the text. Although they are supposed to be following along with the other readers, often they don't because they are nervously skipping ahead to find their portion of the text, anticipating what they will have to read, unable to follow or distracted by the too slow or too rapid reading of their classmate, or bored by the procedure. It is absolutely essential that students read a lot every day. When they're reading a new story, it is important that they read the entire story—often more than once. One way to avoid round-robin reading every day is to have students read the story (or chapter, if the book is longer) silently a few pages at a time and then ask them questions or have them comment on strategies they used. Other appropriate techniques include partner reading, reading softly to themselves while you circulate and "listen in," and popcorn reading, in which students are called on frequently and randomly (often in the middle of a paragraph) to read aloud. If you use any technique in which students have not read the entire selection during their reading group, be sure that they read it in its entirety before or after the reading group.

* **Teach appropriate phrasing and intonation.** Guided oral reading practice and the study of punctuation and grammar can help. To teach appropriate phrasing, see pages 21 and 25. For teaching intonation and punctuation, use some or all of the following. Have students:

    —recite the alphabet as a conversation.

        ABCD? EFG! HI? JKL. MN? OPQ. RST! UVWX. YZ!

—recite the same sentence using different punctuation.

Dogs bark? Dogs bark! Dogs bark.

—practice placing the stress on different words in the same sentence.

I am tired. I *am* tired. I am *tired*.

—practice reading sentences as if talking to a friend.

Studying grammar fosters fluency because grammar alerts the reader to natural phrases in a sentence. For example, being able to identify the subject and the predicate of a sentence is one step in understanding phrase boundaries in text. Also, understanding the role of prepositions and conjunctions adds additional clues to phrase boundaries. (See Lessons 4, 5, 6, and 7 in Section 4 for more grammar activities.)

✳ ***Conduct 2-minute drills to underline or locate a word*** containing a specific sound-spelling (i.e., words with *sh*), a specific syllable or syllable type in a multisyllabic word (i.e., open syllables), or a specific spelling pattern (i.e., words with *-ake*) in an array or short passage (Moats, 1998). This will help students rapidly recognize spelling patterns that are common to many words. And it's a lot of fun.

✳ ***Motivate students to read using incentives, charting, and rewards.*** You want to encourage students to practice reading for long enough periods of time to build accuracy and then automaticity in decoding. *Scholastic Reading Counts!* and *Accelerated Reader* are two popular computer-based motivational systems. Students read books independently, then take tests on the computer. Students earn points for each book read and their test scores are available for teacher viewing or sending to parents.

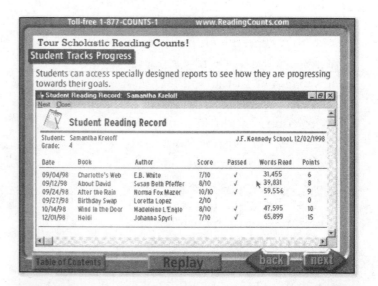

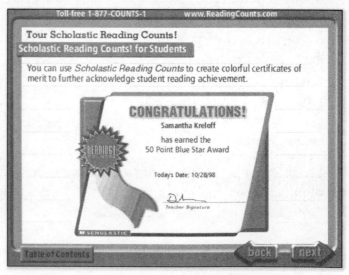

Computer-based reading system

3. Provide reader support
(choral reading and reading while listening)

Readers need to practice reading both orally and silently. Research has shown that oral reading is very important for the developing reader, especially younger children. It appears that young children need to hear themselves read, and they benefit from adult feedback. As well as improving reading, this feedback shows students how highly we adults value the skill of reading. There are several ways to support students' oral reading without evoking the fear and humiliation struggling readers often feel when called on to read aloud. Here are the most popular techniques (always use text at the student's instructional level that enables you to model natural language patterns).

* **Reading aloud simultaneously with a partner or small group.** With this technique, students can "float" in and out as appropriate without feeling singled out. For best results, have students practice reading the selection independently before reading it with the partner or group.

* **Echo reading.** As you read a phrase or sentence in the text, the student repeats it. This continues throughout the text. You can also use a tape recording of the text with pauses for the child to echo the reading.

* **Reader's Theater.** Students choose a favorite part of a book, practice reading it aloud independently until they're confident, and then read it aloud to the class. This reading can be primarily for class enjoyment or it can be part of the student's oral book report. This technique is also terrific for partners or small groups.

* **Choral reading.** Reading together as a group is great for poetry and selections with a distinct pattern. Remind students to "keep your voice with mine" as you read.

✳ ***Paired repeated readings.*** (Koskinen and Blum, 1986). A student reads a short passage three times to a partner and gets feedback. Then the partners switch roles. To avoid frustration, it works best to pair above-level readers with on-level readers and on-level readers with below-level readers.

To maximize student success in working with partners, teach your students how to be excellent partners. Three key partner social skills are (Feldman, 2001):

1. Look. Look at your partner.

2. Lean. Lean toward your partner.

3. Whisper. Use your "12-inch" voice.

✳ ***Books on tape.*** Select and place appropriate books on tape in a classroom listening center. Have students follow along as the book is read, reading with the narrator where possible. Some have criticized this technique for struggling readers because the narrator reads at a pace that is too fast for the student to follow. However, an excellent books-on-tape collection that is sensitive to this issue is READ 180 Audiobooks (Scholastic, 2000). These books contain audio tutors that periodically help students work through comprehension difficulties. (See page 43 for a listing of books and other companies offering audiobooks.)

> ## Pairing Students— Alternate Reading
>
> **1.** Rank and order your students based upon overall literacy proficiency, i.e. highest to lowest.
>
> **2.** Divide the student list into two columns; half being the highest performing students, half being the lower performing students.
>
> **3.** Pair the top reader in column one with the top reader in column two. Continue until all the students have partners. (Example in a 20-Student Classroom: Student 1 and Student 11 form a pair; Student 2 and Student 12 form a pair; and so on.)

4. Use repeated readings of one text

Repeated reading, a popular technique developed by Samuels (1979), has long been recognized as an excellent way to help students achieve fluency. It has been shown to increase reading rate and accuracy and to transfer to new texts. As a child reads a passage at his or her instructional level, the teacher times the reading. The teacher then gives feedback on word-recognition errors and the number of words per minute the child read accurately and records this data on a graph. The child then practices reading the same selection independently or with a partner. The process is repeated and the child's progress plotted on the graph until the child masters the passage. This charting is effective because (1) students become focused on their own mastery of the task and competing with their own past performance, and (2) students have concrete evidence that they are making progress. In addition, repeating the words many

Building Fluency Scholastic Professional Books

times helps students build a large sight-word vocabulary. (See page 50 for more on repeated readings.)

Students who resist rereading selections need incentives. Besides simply telling the student that rereading is a part of the important practice one does to become a better reader, you might motivate her by having her:

—read to a friend, family member, or pet

—read to a student in a lower grade

—read into a tape recorder to record the session

—set a reading-rate goal for a given passage and try to exceed that goal in successive readings

—prepare to perform a reader's theater version of a selection.

Note: This technique is NOT recommended for students already reading fluently.

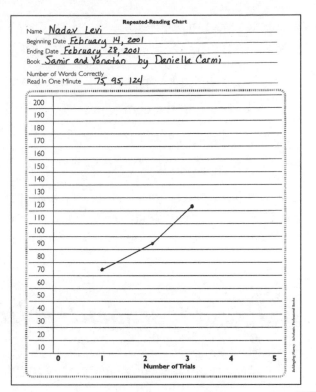

Repeated-Reading Chart

Name Nadav Levi
Beginning Date February 14, 2001
Ending Date February 28, 2001
Book Samir and Yonatan by Daniella Carmi

Number of Words Correctly
Read In One Minute 75, 95, 124

5. Cue phrase boundaries in text

One of the characteristics of proficient (fluent) readers is the ability to group words together in meaningful units—syntactically appropriate phrases. "Proficient reading is characterized not only by fast and accurate word recognition, but also by readers' word chunking or phrasing behavior while reading connected discourse (Rasinski, 1994)." Students who are having trouble with comprehension may not be putting words together in meaningful phrases or chunks as they read. Their oral reading is characterized by a choppy, word-by-word delivery that impedes comprehension. These students need instruction in phrasing written text into appropriate segments.

One way to help students learn to recognize and use natural English phrase boundaries—and thus improve their phrasing, fluency, and comprehension—is **phrase-cued text** practice. Phrase-cued text is a short passage marked by a slash (or some other visual) at the end of each phrase break. The longer pause at the end of the sentence is marked by a double slash (//).

Here's an example:

> In the summer/I like/to swim/at the beach.//
>
> Although it's very hot/I like the idea/
>
> of being in the cool water/
>
> all day.// Summer truly is/
>
> my favorite time/of the year.//

The teacher models good oral reading, and students practice with the marked text. Later, students apply their skills to the same text, unmarked. Have students practice the skill orally for 10 minutes daily. See page 25 for a phrase-cued text lesson and sample texts you can use.

6. Provide students with easy reading materials

Students need an enormous amount of individualized reading practice in decodable materials that are not too difficult (Beck and Juel, 1995; Samuels, Schermer, and Reinking, 1992). Decodable materials are those in which a high percentage of the words can be sounded out by the student based on the phonics skills formerly taught to and practiced by the student. I recommend at least 30 minutes of independent reading every day. Some should occur in school, and some can occur at home. Fluency develops through a great deal of practice in reading stories in which students can use sound-spelling (phonics) strategies (as opposed to contextual strategies—trying to figure out words using one or two letters and sentence or picture clues) to figure out a majority of the unfamiliar words. In the early grades there must be a match between instruction in phonics and reading practice—hence the need for practice stories that are decodable. This match encourages students to adopt sound-spelling strategies and at the same time, through extensive practice reading story after story after story, it leads to fluent reading.

It is critical that practice reading materials be at a child's independent or instructional reading level, NOT at the child's frustrational level. (See next page.) In other words, the student's reading accuracy (the proportion of words read correctly) should be above 90%. During individualized practice, students may be reading at different levels. They read aloud "quietly" to themselves as the teacher walks around listening to each child for a minute or so while still monitoring the group as a whole. Students need time to figure out unfamiliar words through phonic patterns. Expecting students to read fluently when they are not fluent only encourages guessing and memorization.

Building Fluency Scholastic Professional Books

Fluency Intervention

For students who are falling below established fluency norms, choose from the fluency-building activities in Section 4 to provide additional instruction and practice. Some easy-to-instate classroom practices include the following:

* Pinpoint the particular areas of weakness to target instruction.

* Provide ample opportunities to read decodable text and high-interest, easy-reading materials.

* Establish regular partner rereading practice.

* Provide many opportunities for reading and rereading phrase-cued text.

* Set up a Listening Center where students listen to and practice imitating passages of increasing length and complexity.

One recommended fluency intervention program is Read Naturally—a supplemental program to improve reading fluency. For additional information, contact 1-800-788-4085 or www.readnaturally.com.

How to Fit Fluency Into Your Schedule

In order for students to benefit from fluency instruction, it must be daily and ongoing. Below are some suggestions for using the lessons in the next section to incorporate fluency instruction into your regular reading instructional time.

* Conduct short 10-minute lessons twice a week. These lessons can occur at the end of your reading block, but before students engage in silent or partner reading. Choose from the lessons provided in this section. Most can and should be repeated throughout the year. A sample monthly schedule is provided below.

* Provide 30 minutes each day for silent reading—both in class and at home. A portion of this time should include repeated readings of previously read selections. It may also include partner reading.

* Assess each student's fluency rate every 6–8 weeks and help each student establish personal fluency goals.

* Establish fluency checklists for each student. Have students record their reading rate (WCPM) and books read in a specified time period, such as one grading period.

Sample Monthly Fluency Schedule

	Monday	Tuesday	Wednesday	Thursday	Friday
Week 1*	**Fluency Lesson:** Model Phrasing	**Paired Reading:** This week's reading selection	**Fluency Lesson:** Model Intonation	**Repeated Reading:** This week's reading selection	**Assess Fluency Rate** of 5–7 students and set fluency goals**
Week 2*	**Fluency Lesson:** Model Intonation Using Prepositions	**Paired Reading:** This week's reading selection	**Fluency Lesson:** Model Phrasing Using Prepositions	**Repeated Reading:** This week's reading selection	**Assess Fluency Rate** of 5–7 students, set fluency goals
Week 3*	**Fluency Lesson:** Phrase-Cued Text	**Paired Reading:** This week's reading selection	**Fluency Lesson:** Phrase-Cued Text	**Repeated Reading:** This week's reading selection	**Assess Fluency Rate** of 5–7 students, set fluency goals
Week 4*	**Fluency Lesson:** Speed Drill, High Frequency Syllables	**Paired Reading:** This week's reading selection	**Fluency Lesson:** Speed Drill, High Frequency Syllables	**Repeated Reading:** This week's reading selection	**Assess Fluency Rate** of 5–7 students, set fluency goals

* Each day, students should have opportunities to listen to audiobooks in your classroom Listening Center. Cycle students through the center so that each student has 1 or 2 opportunities to visit the center each week.

** Other students engage in repeated readings of this week's selection or read books at their independent reading level.

Section 4

12 Quick-and-Easy Fluency Lessons

Lesson 1

Phrase-Cued Text Practice

Prepare marked and unmarked copies of a phrase-cued text passage. (See page 21 for an explanation.) Distribute copies of the text passage. (See attached samples.)

Have students follow along as you model reading the marked passage using appropriate phrasing and intonation. Then read the text chorally. Have the students read the passage multiple times. Provide appropriate feedback. On subsequent days:

◆ Have students chorally read the marked passage first as a group, then in pairs. Ask students to practice reading the passage independently.

Building Fluency Scholastic Professional Books

◆ Distribute the unmarked version of the passage and ask students to read it independently.

◆ Meet with each student individually and ask him or her to read the unmarked passage. Note phrasing, appropriate pauses, expression, and reading rate. Record the results in each student's Assessment Portfolio.

Phrase-Cued Text Weekly Practice Sessions

Use the following routine for phrase-cued text practice sessions, which should take about 10 minutes a day, several times a week. Select passages on each child's instructional reading level. Make two copies of the passage. On one copy, mark the natural phrase boundaries; leave the other copy unmarked.

DAY 1

1. Select, copy, and distribute a marked text passage (approximately 100–250 words) written at the reading level of a group of students. Explain the format, and tell students that good phrasing will improve their comprehension. Assure them that, with practice, they will get used to reading from marked text.

2. Model reading the marked text aloud as students use their copies to follow along silently. Do this two or three times. Invite students to comment on what they observed about your phrasing and expression.

3. Have students use the marked text to read aloud chorally. They will have additional opportunities to practice throughout the week.

DAY 2

1. Again model reading aloud the marked text.

2. Have students chorally read aloud from copies of their marked text two or three times. Encourage students to comment on their reading and give them your feedback. Also discuss the content of the passage.

3. Have students practice reading aloud the marked text in pairs or small groups.

Encourage them to exchange constructive feedback.

DAY 3

1. Have students use the marked text to read aloud chorally.

2. Follow up by having students practice reading aloud in pairs or small groups.

3. You may wish to have students tape-record themselves, so they can assess their own reading.

4. Encourage students to find opportunities during the day to practice reading their marked text.

DAY 4

1. Distribute the unmarked version of the text.

2. Ask each student to read aloud the passage without the phrases marked. Give each student feedback on his or her reading.

3. Have students practice reading the unmarked text in pairs. They may also tape-record themselves and compare their various readings.

DAY 5

1. Meet with each student individually. Ask him or her to read the unmarked version of the text. Note phrasing, appropriate pauses, expression, and reading rate. Give the student positive feedback.

2. Encourage students to take the passage home and read it to an adult.

Building Fluency   Scholastic Professional Books

Name _____ Date _____

Pass It On!
by Bill E. Neder

All the kids/ were playing.//
"It is my birthday!"/ Pam announced/ to them.//
Meg whispered/ to Tom,// "Let's get Pam/ a hat.// Pass it on."//
Tom whispered/ to Bev,// "We're getting Pam/ a cat.// Pass it on."//
Bev whispered/ to Bob,// "We're giving Pam/ a mat.// Pass it on."//
Bob heard,/ "We're getting Pam/ a bat."//
After playing,/ all the kids/ went home.//
Meg made Pam/ a neat hat.//
Tom found Pam/ a new cat.//
Bev made Pam/ a small mat.//
Bob got Pam/ a big bat.//
Then they all/ went over/ to see Pam.//
Pam got/ so many things!// She recited/ all their names.//
"A hat,/ a cat,/ a mat,/ and a bat!"// Pam announced,// "I am/ so happy!"//

Pass It On!
by Bill E. Neder

All the kids were playing.
"It is my birthday!" Pam announced to them.
Meg whispered to Tom, "Let's get Pam a hat. Pass it on."
Tom whispered to Bev, "We're getting Pam a cat. Pass it on."
Bev whispered to Bob, "We're giving Pam a mat. Pass it on."
Bob heard, "We're getting Pam a bat."
After playing, all the kids went home.
Meg made Pam a neat hat.
Tom found Pam a new cat.
Bev made Pam a small mat.
Bob got Pam a big bat.
Then they all went over to see Pam.
Pam got so many things! She recited all their names.
"A hat, a cat, a mat, and a bat!" Pam announced, "I am so happy!"

Name _____ Date _____

A Man With an Idea

by Dena Ryan

Thomas Alva Edison/ invented many things/ that are still in use/ today.// He had/ good ideas.// When Edison had ideas,/ he worked on them.// He would try/ many things.// The information he got/ from testing his ideas/ was the way/ he invented things.//

This is the story/ of a man/ named Levi Hutchins.// He lived in Concord, New Hampshire,/ over 200 years ago.//One day,/ Levi looked/ at his clock.// He was curious/ about how it worked.// So/ he opened it up.// There was a gear/ in the clock.// There were other things.// Soon/ Levi could see/ how the clock worked.//

"I'm going to make/ a clock,"/ Levi said.// "I am going to work/ on a clock/ that rings out.// The big clocks with bells/ ring out,/ but/ men ring the bells.// No one/ is going to ring/ the bell in my clock."//

Levi got to work.// He had to try many things/ to get his clock to work,/ but/ he had patience.// Soon/ he had/ what he wanted.//

Then/ Levi sat and waited.// Would his clock ring?// It did ring!// Levi had invented/ the first alarm clock!//

Levi let his friends/ hear his clock.// They liked the ringing,/ and were amazed/ at how the clock worked.//

Levi's clock/ was not like/ the alarm clocks we use now.// It could not be set,/ and/ it could not be changed.// Soon/ other people made better alarm clocks,/ but/ Levi's idea/ is still ringing/ in our ears.//

A Man With an Idea

by Dena Ryan

Thomas Alva Edison invented many things that are still in use today. He had good ideas. When Edison had ideas, he worked on them. He would try many things. The information he got from testing his ideas was the way he invented things.

This is the story of a man named Levi Hutchins. He lived in Concord, New Hampshire, over 200 years ago. One day, Levi looked at his clock. He was curious about how it worked. So he opened it up. There was a gear in the clock. There were other things. Soon Levi could see how the clock worked.

"I'm going to make a clock," Levi said. "I am going to work on a clock that rings out. The big clocks with bells ring out, but men ring the bells. No one is going to ring the bell in my clock."

Levi got to work. He had to try many things to get his clock to work, but he had patience. Soon he had what he wanted.

Then Levi sat and waited. Would his clock ring? It did ring! Levi had invented the first alarm clock!

Levi let his friends hear his clock. They liked the ringing, and were amazed at how the clock worked.

Levi's clock was not like the alarm clocks we use now. It could not be set, and it could not be changed. Soon other people made better alarm clocks, but Levi's idea is still ringing in our ears.

Name _____ Date _____

The Mouse Who Learned to Fly
by T. Ernesto Bethancourt

Ichi, the mouse,/ was running for life.// Overhead,/ he heard the scream/ of the hawk.// He saw the shadow/ of the great bird/ as it came rushing toward him.// With only seconds to spare,/ he dived into the hole/ in the ground/ that led to his underground home.//

"Ichi!" cried his mate,/ Harumi.// "What happened?// Are you all right?"//

"A . . . hawk,"/ he gasped.// "It almost got me.// And/ I lost all the seeds/ for our din-ner.// I'm so sorry."//

"It's enough/ that you are safe,"/ Harumi said.// "But/ we must have food.// We have babies/ on the way."//

"I haven't forgotten,"/ Ichi said.// "But/ what am I to do?// In the day,/ when I search for food,// there are foxes, cats, and hawks.// At night,/ there are the owls.// I must do something."//

Ichi sat in a corner/ and began to think.// Harumi began to tidy up their nest/ and the soft bed of grasses she had made/ for when their babies would arrive.// Suddenly,/ Ichi gave a loud cry/ that made Harumi jump/ in surprise.//

"I've got it!"/ Ichi cried.// "We will speak/ to Amateratsu.// She is the goddess/ of the sun/ and all living creatures.// It will be/ a long journey.// Soon/ as it is dark,/ we will begin."//

For weeks,/ Ichi and Harumi traveled,/ day and night.// They were often hungry/ and always,/ there were foxes and hawks by day/ and owls by night,/ ready to pounce on them.// Finally,/ just as the sun was setting/ on the highest mountaintop,/ they found Amateratsu.//

She was the most beautiful thing/ Ichi and Harumi had ever seen.// Her kimono was made up of/ all the colors/ of the sunrise.// Her hair and eyes/ were dark as night.// Though he was frightened,/ Ichi approached the goddess.//

"Oh,/ most wonderful Amateratsu,"/ Ichi said,/ "my wife and I need your help . . ."// His voice trailed off.// He was shaking badly.// The goddess smiled,/ and suddenly/ Ichi was no longer afraid.// She reached down/ and took the little mouse/ in the palm of her hand.// "I know why you have come,/ little one,"/ she said,/ "for I know all things/ about all living creatures.// You and Harumi/ have shown a great courage,/ seeking me out.// There have been dangers/ every step of the way.// You have braved these/ for the sake/ of your chil-dren to come."// She reached down/ and picked up Harumi.// "You,/ little mother-to-be,/ are most dear to me,/ for I am mother/ to all creatures."//

The goddess sat Harumi down/ and took Ichi/ in both hands.// Ever so gently/ she began to tug on/ the folds of skin and fur/ from Ichi's paws/ to his chest.// "Ouch!"/

The Mouse Who Learned to Fly (Cont.)

said Ichi.//

"Hush!"/ the goddess said.// "There is no gain/ without a little pain."//

"But/ what am I gaining?"/ asked Ichi.//

"Patience,/ little one.// You will soon see."// She continued tugging.// Ichi felt very strange/ indeed.// He looked down.//

"My tail!"/ he cried.// "My beautiful tail is gone!"//

"You will not be needing it/ anymore,"/ said Amateratsu.// She began to tug/ at Ichi's ears.// "Hmmm.// These will need/ a bit of work."//

In a short time,/ the goddess' work was finished.// She waved a hand/ and magically,/ a tall mirror appeared.// Holding Ichi between her fingers,/ she spread out his front legs/ and held him up/ to the mirror.//

Ichi was filled with wonder.// From the ends of his front paws/ to his hind legs,/ he now had/ a pair of leathery wings!// His ears/ were no longer round,/ but rose up/ in sharp points.// Then,/ Amateratsu tossed Ichi/ high into the air.// "Fly,/ little one!"/ she commanded.// And fly,/ Ichi did.// He soared,/ he dived,/ and he swooped.// He shouted for joy,/ but instead of his regular voice,/ out came a high-pitched squeal.// He was so surprised/ that he almost flew/ into the goddess.// "This is wonderful!"/ he cried.//

"Your wings come at a price,/ Ichi,"/ the goddess said.// "You will no longer walk/ on the ground.// Instead of ripe seeds,/ you will live/ on bugs you catch."//

"I can live with that,"/ said Ichi.//

"There is more,"/ the goddess continued.// "You will live/ in a cave/ and sleep by day.// You will sleep/ hanging upside down.// You will no more see my smile/ as I rise from the sea/ in the east/ each day."//

A small tear/ ran down Ichi's face.//

"Not ever?"/ he asked.//

"Well,/ perhaps for a few seconds/ at the end of the day.// But/ you will no longer fear/ the hawk and fox.// You will be a cleverer flier/ than the owl."// She reached down/ and picked up Harumi.// "Now/ to take care of you,/ little mother-to-be."//

The goddess' hands flew/ over Harumi's tiny body.// In moments,/ she joined Ichi,/ flying through the air.// "Oh,/ thank you,/ most wonderful Amateratsu!"/ they said.//

"There is one more thing,"/ the goddess said.// "You are no longer mice.// You need a new name.// I shall call you komori."// Saying this,/ the goddess disappeared.//

Komori are bats,/ of course.// And to this day,/ the children/ of Hamuri and Ichi/ fly out of their cave/ just as the sun sets.// In this short moment,/ they are able to see and feel/ the warmth of Amateratsu's smile.//

Name _____ Date _____

The Mouse Who Learned to Fly

by T. Ernesto Bethancourt

Ichi, the mouse, was running for life. Overhead, he heard the scream of the hawk. He saw the shadow of the great bird as it came rushing toward him. With only seconds to spare, he dived into the hole in the ground that led to his underground home.

"Ichi!" cried his mate, Harumi. "What happened? Are you all right?"

"A . . . hawk," he gasped. "It almost got me. And I lost all the seeds for our dinner. I'm so sorry."

"It's enough that you are safe," Harumi said. "But we must have food. We have babies on the way."

"I haven't forgotten," Ichi said. "But what am I to do? In the day, when I search for food, there are foxes, cats, and hawks. At night, there are the owls. I must do something."

Ichi sat in a corner and began to think. Harumi began to tidy up their nest and the soft bed of grasses she had made for when their babies would arrive. Suddenly, Ichi gave a loud cry that made Harumi jump in surprise.

"I got it!" Ichi cried. "We will speak to Amateratsu. She is the goddess of the sun and all living creatures. It will be a long journey. Soon as it is dark, we will begin."

For weeks, Ichi and Harumi traveled, day and night. They were often hungry and always there were foxes and hawks by day and owls by night, ready to pounce on them. Finally, just as the sun was setting on the highest mountaintop, they found Amateratsu.

She was the most beautiful thing Ichi and Harumi had ever seen. Her kimono was made up of all the colors of the sunrise. Her hair and eyes were dark as night. Though he was frightened, Ichi approached the goddess.

"Oh, most wonderful Amateratsu," Ichi said, "my wife and I need your help . . ." His voice trailed off. He was shaking badly. The goddess smiled, and suddenly Ichi was no longer afraid. She reached down and took the little mouse in the palm of her hand.

"I know why you have come, little one," she said, "for I know all things about all living creatures. You and Harumi have shown a great courage, seeking me out. There have been dangers every step of the way. You have braved these for the sake of your children to come." She reached down and picked up Harumi. "You, little mother-to-be, are most dear to me, for I am mother to all creatures."

The goddess sat Harumi down and took Ichi in both hands. Ever so gently she began to tug on the folds of skin and fur from Ichi's paws to his chest. "Ouch!" said Ichi.

"Hush!" the goddess said. "There is no gain without a little pain."
"But what am I gaining?" asked Ichi.

"Patience, little one. You will soon see." She continued tugging. Ichi felt very strange indeed. He looked down.

The Mouse Who Learned to Fly (Cont.)

"My tail!" he cried. "My beautiful tail is gone!"

"You will not be needing it anymore," said Amateratsu. She began to tug at Ichi's ears. "Hmmm. These will need a bit of work."

In a short time, the goddess' work was finished. She waved a hand and magically, a tall mirror appeared. Holding Ichi between her fingers, she spread out his front legs and held him up to the mirror.

Ichi was filled with wonder. From the ends of his front paws to his hind legs, he now had a pair of leathery wings! His ears were no longer round, but rose up in sharp points. Then, Amateratsu tossed Ichi high into the air. "Fly, little one!" she commanded.

And fly, Ichi did. He soared, he dived, and he swooped. He shouted for joy, but instead of his regular voice, out came a high-pitched squeal. He was so surprised that he almost flew into the goddess. "This is wonderful!" he cried.

"Your wings come at a price, Ichi," the goddess said. "You will no longer walk on the ground. Instead of ripe seeds, you will live on bugs you catch."

"I can live with that," said Ichi.

"There is more," the goddess continued. "You will live in a cave and sleep by day. You will sleep hanging upside down. You will no more see my smile as I rise from the sea in the east each day."

A small tear ran down Ichi's face.

"Not ever?" he asked.

"Well, perhaps for a few seconds at the end of the day. But you will no longer fear the hawk and fox. You will be a cleverer flier than the owl." She reached down and picked up Harumi. "Now to take care of you, little mother-to-be."

The goddess' hands flew over Harumi's tiny body. In moments, she joined Ichi, flying through the air. "Oh, thank you, most wonderful Amateratsu!" they said.

"There is one more thing," the goddess said. "You are no longer mice. You need a new name. I shall call you komori." Saying this, the goddess disappeared.

Komori are bats, of course. And to this day, the children of Hamuri and Ichi fly out of their cave just as the sun sets. In this short moment, they are able to see and feel the warmth of Amateratsu's smile.

Name _____ Date _____

The King of Soccer!

by Camilla Gutierrez

Edson Arantes do Nasciemento/ was born in Brazil.// His dad/ was a pro soccer player.// In Brazil/, soccer players are often known/ by their nicknames,/ and Edson's dad/ was known as Dondinho.//

When Edson was four,/ his family moved/ to the city/ of Bauru.// It was there/ Edson got his nick-name.// Kids on the street/ started calling him Pelé (pay-lay).// Some say/ the name came/ from a game called pelada.// Wherever it came from,/ it was a good choice.// Pelé is Hawaii's name/ for the Goddess/ of the Volcano.// And like a volcano,/ Pelé's power and talent/ were about to erupt/ on the world!//

Pelé grew up shoeless/ in hand-me-down clothes.// When it was cold,/ Pelé,/ his mom, dad, and younger sister and brother/ huddled around a wood-burning stove/ in the kitchen.// They slept/ on the floor/ to stay warm.// But/ Pelé never thought he was poor.// "I was always happy/ in Bauru,"/ he once said.//

The neighborhood/ was full of children.// They played all day.// Afternoons were best of all!// The big kids/ got out of school,/ and Pelé and his friends/ watched them play soccer.// As they grew,/ they tried to join games,/ but the older boys/ still shooed them away.//

The younger boys decided/ to form a team/ of their own.// They had no money/ for a ball,/ so/ they did what other kids did.// They put newspaper and rags/ in a big sock/ and rolled it/ into a "ball."// Lashed together with string,/ it worked pretty well.//

While soccer was always their favorite game,/ Pelé and his friends/ did other things.// They swam/ in the river./ They watched planes/ take off and land.// They collected and sold stuff,/ and they got into trouble.//

Young Pelé often caused some problems/ for his mom.// He didn't do his homework./ His soccer kicks/ broke windows.// One rainy day/ she caught him/ before he could go out.// She sat him down/ and made him do/ his homework.// Pelé and his friends/ had built caves/ at a construction site.// The other boys/ were all out playing in them.// Pelé was mad!/ It was such fun/ to be dry and warm/ inside a tunnel/ while the rain poured down outside!//

As Pelé sat/ staring at his homework,/ he heard a friend/ call his name.// The cave had collapsed.// One of the boys/ was inside.// People from the neighborhood/ dug and dug.// In the end,/ it was all for nothing.// The boy died/ while they were digging.//

Pelé felt terrible and responsible.// He had been/ one of the builders/ of the caves.// He felt funny/ about not being there that day.// If his mom had let him go out to play,/ he might have been hurt.//

Pelé wanted to be a soccer player/ like his dad.// He watched his games.// He asked questions/ and had his dad demonstrate moves.// Dondinho taught Pelé/ how to dribble and kick.// Then,/ he'd play goalie.// Pelé would try/ to get the ball past him.// He seldom could.// Dondinho always seemed to know/ where to be/ to block it.//

Pelé could have kept his dad's advice/ to himself,/ but he didn't.// Soccer is a team sport.// So whenev-er he could,/ he passed on his dad's advice/ to his teammates.//

When Pelé was nine,/ he and his friends earned money/ to get a soccer ball and some uniforms.// They couldn't afford shoes,/ but other kids' teams in Bauru/ played shoeless, too.// One day,/ a soccer fan named Joe Milk/ bought them shoes.// The shoes pinched their feet.// They couldn't control the ball/ with shoes on,/ so the boys/ took them off.// That was bad/ because the city was holding a competition,/ and Joe said they had to wear shoes.// They put them back on.// Eventually,/ Pelé found something out.// With shoes on,/ he could kick the ball/ with his toes/ as well as the sides/ of his feet.// Shoes are good,/ he decided.//

The King of Soccer! (Cont.)

When he was eleven,/ a coach named "de Brito"/ noticed him.// De Brito had played/ in the World Cup!// He knew a great soccer player/ when he saw one.// He put Pelé/ on the city's junior team.// Within three years,/ Pelé was a star player.//

One day,/ de Brito asked Pelé's parents/ if he could take him/ to the city of Santos/ to try out for the pro team there.// Santos was a city/ over 200 miles away,/ and Pelé was only fifteen.// It was hard,/ but they let him go.//

The day of the tryout,/ de Brito told the team directors,/ "This boy will be/ the greatest soccer player/ in the world."// The Santos coach took Pelé,/ but he put him/ on the junior team.// Pelé was disappointed.// He was ready/ for the first team,/ but the coach/ didn't know it.// His father had told him long ago/ that he needed more than talent/ to be a superstar.// You needed luck.//

Luck came/ when a nearby team needed players/ for a game.// Pelé played so well/ the Santos coach couldn't help noticing.// So when Pelé was 17,/ he was on Santos's first team.//

Scores in soccer/ are usually low.// Even so,/ Pelé scored 17 goals in 1957!// It was a league record.// A year later,/ he played in the World Cup!//

Pelé's performance/ in the World Cup/ was a triumph!// The quarter-final game/ was against Wales.// The game was scoreless/ when Pelé banked a shot/ off a Welsh player.// As the ball bounced back,/ Pelé booted it again,/ this time/ into the net!// Brazil won one to nothing.//

In the match with Sweden,/ Pelé made two/ of the five goals.// Brazil won 5–2.// Pelé stunned Sweden's star player.// He said of Pelé,/ "After the fifth goal,/ I wanted to applaud him."//

Brazil came home/ with its first World Cup title.// Pelé was a celebrity,/ and he was not yet 18!//

Pelé played for Santos/ for 17 years.// In 1969,/ he scored his 1,000th goal/ before a roaring crowd.// During all that time,/ he helped Brazil/ win three out of four World Cups!// After the 1970 competition,/ one Italian opponent said,/ "I thought:/ he is made of flesh and bones/ like me./ I was wrong."//

Pelé's opponents/ were constantly awed/ at his skills.// One goalie couldn't take it.// He couldn't stop Pelé's shots.// He was so embarrassed/ that he ran off the field/ in front of 20,000 people.//

In 1974,/ Pelé retired.// He was only 33.// He loved the game.// But/ he wanted to spend more time/ with his wife and children.// His retirement didn't last long.// There was one more challenge/ he had to face.//

Soccer is the most popular game/ in the world,/ but people in the United States/ were more interested in football, basketball, and baseball.// Soccer teams thought:/ Pelé draws huge crowds worldwide.// If we can get him/ to play for a U.S. team,/ we'd get Americans interested/ in soccer.// This was a challenge/ to Pelé,/ so he signed/ with the New York Cosmos.//

Many of Pelé's Cosmos teammates/ were not very good.// They hadn't played/ all their lives.// They lacked skill and experience,/ but Pelé never complained.// He shared what he knew/ and helped them get better,/ just as he had years before/ in his hometown.//

The plan worked.// Soccer crowds doubled and tripled.// Great players/ from other countries/ came to the U.S.// If soccer's king could play/ in the U.S.,/ they could, too.//

Pelé played his last pro game/ in 1977:/ Cosmos vs. Santos.// Pelé played half the game/ for each of his teams.// When the game ended,/ Pelé took off his number 10 Santos shirt/ and gave it/ to the Santos coach.// Then,/ he ran around the field/ in a final victory lap.// As he ran,/ the crowd shouted his name.//

Pelé,/ the king of soccer,/ was not only the greatest soccer player/ the world had ever seen.// He was also loved/ by soccer fans everywhere.//

Name _____ Date _____

The King of Soccer!

by Camilla Gutierrez

Edson Arantes do Nasciemento was born in Brazil. His dad was a pro soccer player. In Brazil, soccer players are often known by their nicknames, and Edson's dad was known as Dondinho.

When Edson was four, his family moved to the city of Bauru. It was there Edson got his nickname. Kids on the street started calling him Pelé (pay-lay). Some say the name came from a game called pelada. Wherever it came from, it was a good choice. Pelé is Hawaii's name for the Goddess of the Volcano. And like a volcano, Pelé's power and talent were about to erupt on the world!

Pelé grew up shoeless in hand-me-down clothes. When it was cold, Pelé, his mom, dad, and younger sister and brother huddled around a wood-burning stove in the kitchen. They slept on the floor to stay warm. But Pelé never thought he was poor. "I was always happy in Bauru," he once said.

The neighborhood was full of children. They played all day. Afternoons were best of all! The big kids got out of school, and Pelé and his friends watched them play soccer. As they grew, they tried to join games, but the older boys still shooed them away.

The younger boys decided to form a team of their own. They had no money for a ball, so they did what other kids did. They put newspaper and rags in a big sock and rolled it into a "ball." Lashed together with string, it worked pretty well.

While soccer was always their favorite game, Pelé and his friends did other things. They swam in the river. They watched planes take off and land. They collected and sold stuff, and they got into trouble.

Young Pelé often caused some problems for his mom. He didn't do his homework. His soccer kicks broke windows. One rainy day she caught him before he could go out. She sat him down and made him do his homework. Pelé and his friends had built caves at a construction site. The other boys were all out playing in them. Pelé was mad! It was such fun to be dry and warm inside a tunnel while the rain poured down outside!

As Pelé sat staring at his homework, he heard a friend call his name. The cave had collapsed. One of the boys was inside. People from the neighborhood dug and dug. In the end, it was all for nothing. The boy died while they were digging.

Pelé felt terrible and responsible. He had been one of the builders of the caves. He felt funny about not being there that day. If his mom had let him go out to play, he might have been hurt.

Pelé wanted to be a soccer player like his dad. He watched his games. He asked questions and had his dad demonstrate moves. Dondinho taught Pelé how to dribble and kick. Then, he'd play goalie. Pelé would try to get the ball past him. He seldom could. Dondinho always seemed to know where to be to block it.

Pelé could have kept his dad's advice to himself, but he didn't. Soccer is a team sport. So whenever he could, he passed on his dad's advice to his teammates.

When Pelé was nine, he and his friends earned money to get a soccer ball and some uniforms. They couldn't afford shoes, but other kids' teams in Bauru played shoeless, too. One day, a soccer fan named Joe Milk bought them shoes. The shoes pinched their feet. They couldn't control the ball with shoes on, so the boys took them off. That was bad because the city was holding a competition, and Joe said they had to wear shoes. They put them back on. Eventually, Pelé found something out. With shoes on, he could kick the ball with his toes as well as the sides of his feet. Shoes are good, he decided.

The King of Soccer! (Cont.)

When he was eleven, a coach named "de Brito" noticed him. De Brito had played in the World Cup! He knew a great soccer player when he saw one. He put Pelé on the city's junior team. Within three years, Pelé was a star player.

One day, de Brito asked Pelé's parents if he could take him to the city of Santos to try out for the pro team there. Santos was a city over 200 miles away, and Pelé was only fifteen. It was hard, but they let him go.

The day of the tryout, de Brito told the team directors, "This boy will be the greatest soccer player in the world." The Santos coach took Pelé, but he put him on the junior team. Pelé was disappointed. He was ready for the first team, but the coach didn't know it. His father had told him long ago that he needed more than talent to be a superstar. He needed luck.

Luck came when a nearby team needed players for a game. Pelé played so well the Santos coach couldn't help noticing. So when Pelé was 17, he was on Santos's first team.

Scores in soccer are usually low. Even so, Pelé scored 17 goals in 1957! It was a league record. A year later, he played in the World Cup!

Pelé's performance in the World Cup was a triumph! The quarter-final game was against Wales. The game was scoreless when Pelé banked a shot off a Welsh player. As the ball bounced back, Pelé booted it again, this time into the net! Brazil won one to nothing.

In the match with Sweden, Pelé made two of the five goals. Brazil won 5–2. Pelé stunned Sweden's star player. He said of Pelé, "After the fifth goal, I wanted to applaud him."

Brazil came home with its first World Cup title. Pelé was a celebrity, and he was not yet 18!

Pelé played for Santos for 17 years. In 1969, he scored his 1,000th goal before a roaring crowd. During all that time, he helped Brazil win three out of four World Cups! After the 1970 competition, one Italian opponent said, "I thought: he is made of flesh and bones like me. I was wrong."

Pelé opponents were constantly awed at his skills. One goalie couldn't take it. He couldn't stop Pelé's shots. He was so embarrassed that he ran off the field in front of 20,000 people.

In 1974, Pelé retired. He was only 33. He loved the game. But he wanted to spend more time with his wife and children. His retirement didn't last long. There was one more challenge he had to face.

Soccer is the most popular game in the world, but people in the United States were more interested in football, basketball, and baseball. Soccer teams thought: Pelé draws huge crowds worldwide. If we can get him to play for a U.S. team, we'd get Americans interested in soccer. This was a challenge to Pelé, so he signed with the New York Cosmos.

Many of Pelé's Cosmos teammates were not very good. They hadn't played all their lives. They lacked skill and experience, but Pelé never complained. He shared what he knew and helped them get better, just as he had years before in his hometown.

The plan worked. Soccer crowds doubled and tripled. Great players from other countries came to the U.S. If soccer's king could play in the U.S., they could, too.

Pelé played his last pro game in 1977: Cosmos vs. Santos. Pelé played half the game for each of his teams. When the game ended, Pelé took off his number 10 Santos shirt and gave it to the Santos coach. Then, he ran around the field in a final victory lap. As he ran, the crowd shouted his name.

Pelé, the king of soccer, was not only the greatest soccer player the world had ever seen. He was also loved by soccer fans everywhere.

Name _____ Date _____

Our Nation's Capital

by Doris Licameli

After the revolution,/ America needed a capital city.//

"Make it New York City,"/ some said.//

"Philadelphia!"/ demanded others.//

George Washington made the decision.//

He picked an area/ on the Potomac River.// It was between the states to the north/ and to the south.//

The capital city/ became known as Washington,/ District of Columbia.//

At first,/ the area was a wilderness.// Water from the Potomac River/ made it muddy, too.// Huge numbers of mosquitoes/ grew there/ and made people very sick.// So/ swamps and creeks/ had to be drained.//

After things improved,/ Pierre L'Enfant was hired/ to plan the new city.// He chose the perfect spot/ for the Capitol building.// It was called Jenkins' Hill.//

"This hill looks like a pedestal/ waiting for a monument,"/ he thought.//

The President's House/ was to be built/ on a hill, too.//

Mr. L'Enfant made plans/ for broad avenues.//

He designed/ pretty gardens and parks, too.// Then/ trouble came his way.// He was fired/ before anything was built.//

The plans were saved/ over time.// A hundred years later,/ they inspired new planners.//

Now/ the skyline of the capital/ has grown.//

Many fine buildings/ have risen.// Some look like Greek and Roman temples.// Our form of government/ was born in ancient Greece and Rome.//

Unique monuments/ have been built.// They honor special presidents.// They honor war heroes, too.//

Washington, D.C. has become/ an exciting place.// Visitors come/ from around the world.//

The National Mall is a landmark.// It is a center/ of great public places.//

We can see the government/ at work.//

We can visit/ magnificent museums.// History and science come alive/ for us/ inside them.//

Gardens and parks are everywhere.// There is much beauty/ to admire.//

The most famous address/ in Washington, D.C./ is 1600 Pennsylvania Avenue.// It is the White House.// It is the official home/ of the President/ of the United States.//

Once,/ it was called the President's House.// It was called the President's Palace, too.// It looks/ like a great white palace/ and keeping it that way/ takes 570 gallons of white paint.//

John Adams was the first president/ to live in the White House.// Only six rooms were done/ when he moved in.// Not long after,/ the British burned it down.// It took many years/ to build again.// It was the largest house/ in America.//

Today/ there are 132 rooms/ in the White House.// The president and his family/ live on the second floor.// The president works/ in the Oval Office.// There he manages the business/ of the country.//

The East Room/ is the biggest room/ in the White House.// It is large enough/ for dances and weddings.// President Teddy Roosevelt even held boxing matches/ in the East Room.//

Our Nation's Capital (Cont.)

Some presidents bring along their pets.// The pets aren't only cats and dogs./ Once,/ there was a pony named Macaroni.// He liked to roam/ around the White House gardens.// Old Whiskers,/ a goat,/ lived there, too.//

Only one president/ didn't live in the White House.// That was George Washington.//

People around the world/ recognize the domed capitol building.// On top/ is a statue/ called Freedom.//

No building in Washington, D.C./ may be taller/ than the statue.// Nothing may stand/ above Freedom.//

The Capitol is where the laws are made,/ and the Senate is in its north wing.//

The Rotunda lies/ in the center.// It is a round area/ under the dome.// The Capitol is almost ninety feet/ above the level/ of the Potomac River/ so the view from the windows/ is amazing.//

The Washington Monument/ is about a mile/ from the Capitol.// The Lincoln Memorial/ is more than two miles away.// Both of these landmarks/ can be seen/ from the Capitol.//

The Bureau of Engraving and Printing/ is where paper money/ is made.// A stack of ten-dollar bills/ is on display there.// The bills add up to $1,000,000.00,/ and it's exciting to see/ what a million dollars looks like.//

The Smithsonian Institute/ is known as the Castle.// It's also called "the nation's attic."//

The National Museum of American History/ is another wonderful spot.// It's filled with history and science,/ and there is much to learn.// Kids can learn/ how to harness a mule.//

Curious minds/ can even work/ on science experiments.//

More fun is waiting/ at the National Museum of Natural History.// There are dinosaur skeletons/ and giant squid.// There are amazing displays/ about volcanoes and rocks.//

Part of the museum/ is an insect zoo/ with all kinds of live insects/ from around the world.// Some may be handled/ by anyone brave enough.//

Maybe we'll just watch the tarantulas/ get fed!//

The most visited museum/ in the world/ is the Air and Space Museum.// Here,/ the story of flying/ comes alive.// Some exhibits hang/ from the ceiling.// We can see the first airplane/ to really fly.// We can feel like astronauts/ inside a space module.//

The Lincoln Memorial/ looks like a Greek temple.// It has 36 columns.// There's one column/ for each state/ at the time of Lincoln's death.// The famous huge sculpture of Lincoln/ sits at the center.//

A mural shows an angel/ freeing a slave.//

Lincoln's famous speeches/ are on the walls.// The Memorial is the place/ where Dr. Martin Luther King gave his famous speech.//

President Lincoln was shot/ in the Fords Theater,/ which is still open.// There is a Lincoln museum/ in the basement.// Lincoln died/ in the Peterson House,/ across the street/ from the theater.//

The Washington Monument towers/ over the National Mall.// It has come to represent Washington, D.C.// The monument is made up/ of 36,000 blocks of stone.// There are 897 steps leading/ to the top/ of the monument.// Its elevator takes people/ to the top/ in only 70 seconds.// (So why walk?)// On a clear day/ the view goes for miles.//

Name _____ Date _____

Our Nation's Capital

by Doris Licameli

After the revolution, America needed a capital city.

"Make it New York City," some said.

"Philadelphia!" demanded others.

George Washington made the decision.

He picked an area on the Potomac River. It was between the states to the north and to the south.

The capital city became known as Washington, District of Columbia.

At first, the area was a wilderness. Water from the Potomac River made it muddy, too. Huge numbers of mosquitoes grew there and made people very sick. So swamps and creeks had to be drained.

After things improved, Pierre L'Enfant was hired to plan the new city. He chose the perfect spot for the Capitol building. It was called Jenkins' Hill.

"This hill looks like a pedestal waiting for a monument," he thought.

The President's House was to be built on a hill, too.

Mr. L'Enfant made plans for broad avenues.

He designed pretty gardens and parks, too. Then trouble came his way. He was fired before anything was built.

The plans were saved over time. A hundred years later, they inspired new planners.

Now the skyline of the capital has grown.

Many fine buildings have risen. Some look like Greek and Roman temples. Our form of government was born in ancient Greece and Rome.

Unique monuments have been built. They honor special presidents. The honor war heroes, too.

Washington, D.C. has become an exciting place. Visitors come from around the world.

The National Mall is a landmark. It is a center of great public places.

We can see the government at work.

We can visit magnificent museums. History and science come alive for us inside them.

Gardens and parks are everywhere. There is much beauty to admire.

The most famous address in Washington, D.C. is 1600 Pennsylvania Avenue. It is the White House. It is the official home of the President of the United States.

Once, it was called the President's House. It was called the President's Palace, too. It looks like a great white palace and keeping it that way takes 570 gallons of white paint.

John Adams was the first president to live in the White House. Only six rooms were done when he moved in. Not long after, the British burned it down. It took many years to build again. It was the largest house in America.

Today there are 132 rooms in the White House. The president and his family live on the second floor. The president works in the Oval Office. There he manages the business of the country.

The East Room is the biggest room in the White House. It is large enough for dances and

Our Nation's Capital (Cont.)

weddings. President Teddy Roosevelt even held boxing matches in the East Room.

Some presidents bring along their pets. The pets aren't only cats and dogs. Once, there was a pony named Macaroni. He liked to roam around the White House gardens. Old Whiskers, a goat, lived there, too.

Only one president didn't live in the White House. That was George Washington.

People around the world recognize the domed capitol building. On top is a statue called Freedom.

No building in Washington, D.C. may be taller than the statue. Nothing may stand above Freedom.

The Capitol is where the laws are made, and the Senate is in its north wing.

The Rotunda lies in the center. It is a round area under the dome. The Capitol is almost ninety feet above the level of the Potomac River so the view from the windows is amazing.

The Washington Monument is about a mile from the Capitol. The Lincoln Memorial is more than two miles away. Both of these landmarks can be seen from the Capitol.

The Bureau of Engraving and Printing is where paper money is made. A stack of ten-dollar bills is on display there. The bills add up to $1,000,000.00, and it's exciting to see what a million dollars looks like.

The Smithsonian Institute is known as the Castle. It's also called "the nation's attic."

The National Museum of American History is another wonderful spot. It's filled with history and science, and there is much to learn. Kids can learn how to harness a mule.

Curious minds can even work on science experiments.

More fun is waiting at the National Museum of Natural History. There are dinosaur skeletons and giant squid. There are amazing displays about volcanoes and rocks.

Part of the museum is an insect zoo with all kinds of live insects from around the world. Some may be handled by anyone brave enough.

Maybe we'll just watch the tarantulas get fed!

The most visited museum in the world is the Air and Space Museum. Here, the story of flying comes alive. Some exhibits hang from the ceiling. We can see the first airplane to really fly. We can feel like astronauts inside a space module.

The Lincoln Memorial looks like a Greek temple. It has 36 columns. There's one column for each state at the time of Lincoln's death. The famous huge sculpture of Lincoln sits at the center.

A mural shows an angel freeing a slave.

Lincoln's famous speeches are on the walls. The Memorial is the place where Dr. Martin Luther King, Jr. gave his famous speech.

President Lincoln was shot in the Fords Theater, which is still open. There is a Lincoln museum in the basement. Lincoln died in the Peterson House, across the street from the theater.

The Washington Monument towers over the National Mall. It has come to represent Washington, D.C. The monument is made up of 36,000 blocks of stone. There are 897 steps leading to the top of the monument. Its elevator takes people to the top in only 70 seconds. (So why walk?) On a clear day the view goes for miles.

Lesson 2

Echo Reading

Explain to students that you will model fluent reading. As you read, have students listen for:

* changes in stress and pitch
* pauses
* how you chunk the text

Use the following routine:

1. Choose a passage or page from the week's main reading selection.

2. Read one phrase or sentence at a time, as students follow along in their books.

3. Have students echo your reading. Discuss any difficulties they have. Point out changes in stress and pitch, pauses, and how you chunk text.

4. When you are finished with the passage, have student pairs chorally reread for additional practice.

Echo-Reading Checklist

✔ Point out the raise in voice at the end of a question.

✔ Read an exclamation with strong emotion.

✔ Read dialogue the way it would be spoken.

✔ Chunk text using major parts of sentences, such as subject, predicate, and prepositional phrases.

✔ Pause at the end of a sentence, end of a paragraph, or at a comma.

✔ Note smoothness in reading and correct pronunciation of all words.

Lesson 3

Audiobook Modeling

Explain to students that they will listen to how a good reader reads aloud and use the model to improve their own fluency.

Use the following routine:

1. Select an audiobook on each student's reading level. You may wish to use the audiobook for

the selection you're reading that week (if available from your basal publisher).

2. Have students listen to the recording as they follow along in the corresponding book.

3. Tell students to stop at the end of each page and reread using the same pace, phrasing, and expression as the narrator.

4. Students should repeat this exercise as many times as necessary—until they feel confident in their reading.

5. Finally, have students record their reading on an audiocassette. You may wish to place each student's recording in his or her Assessment Portfolio or in your classroom Listening Center.

Tips for Choosing Audiobooks

✓ Select books that are at or above the students' grade level.

✓ Choose books that are classics, favorites, or on topics of interest to the students. You may even want to choose books related to the science and social studies topics covered in your curriculum, or books of a particular genre.

✓ Choose books rich in language and detail. This will aid students in developing their listening and speaking vocabularies.

✓ Choose both fiction AND nonfiction.

✓ Choose books written by a popular children's author. Encourage students to compare the books.

Lexiles: What Are They?

The Lexile Framework® is a readability measure that is coming into widespread use across the country. It matches students to text and is unique because it uses one measurement—a Lexile measurement—to assess both the level of the reader and the level of the text. For a student, a Lexile Level is a measure of reading comprehension. For a book, a Lexile Level is a measure of text difficulty. When a reader has the same Lexile Level as a book, the student should be able to read the book with approximately 75% comprehension, (e.g., Pablo reads at a 640 Lexile Level and the book *Jerusalem, a City in White* is at the 640 Lexile Level). The Lexile Framework helps teachers:

* more precisely measure a student's reading performance

* accurately assess and monitor achievement

* recommend books and encourage reluctant readers

Building Fluency Scholastic Professional Books

Lexile-Level Chart

Approximate Grade Level	Lexile-Level Ranges	Sample Books
Grade 2	300–600	*Miss Nelson Is Missing* (Allard, 340)
		Fossils Tell of Long Ago (Aliki, 480)
Grade 3	500–800	*Superfudge* (Blume, 560)
		Henry Huggins (Cleary, 670)
Grade 4	600–900	*The Big Wave* (Buck, 790)
Grade 5	700–1000	*Peter Pan* (Barrie, 920)
Grade 6	800–1050	*The Phantom Tollbooth* (Juster, 1000)

Libraries and book clubs around the country are beginning to list the Lexile levels of their books. To check the Lexile levels of your favorite books, go to www.lexile.com and click on "Search" to register.

Audiobooks With Comprehension Models*

	Lexile Level
Back to the Titanic by Beatrice Gormley	710
Beautiful Warrior: The Legend of the Nun's Kung Fu by Emily Arnold McCully	630
Favorite Greek Myths by Mary Pope Osborne	870
For Your Eyes Only! by Joanne Rocklin	670
I Thought My Soul Would Rise and Fly by Joyce Hansen	820
Jonah the Whale by Susan Shreve	740
The Journal of Joshua Loper: A Black Cowboy by Walter Dean Myers	1000
The Last-Place Sports Poems of Jeremy Bloom by Gordon Korman and Bernice Korman	760
The Magnificent Mummy Maker by Elvira Woodruff	800
The Music of Dolphins by Karen Hesse	560
The Ostrich Chase by Moses L. Howard	860
Pacific Crossing by Gary Soto	750
Across the Wide and Lonesome Prairie by Kristiana Gregory	940
Daniel's Story by Carol Matas	720
Flight #116 Is Down by Caroline B. Cooney	710
Local News by Gary Soto	820
The Mighty by Rodman Philbrick	1000
P.S. Longer Letter Later by Paula Danzinger and Ann M. Martin	750
Quake! by Joe Cottonwood	590
Snowbound by David Lavender	890

* Read 180 Audiobooks (Scholastic, 2000).

Audiobooks With Comprehension Models* (cont.)

	Lexile Level
Somewhere in the Darkness by Walter Dean Myers	640
The Star Fisher by Laurence Yep	740
The Stowaway by Kristiana Gregory	820
You Be the Jury by Marvin Miller	770

* Read 180 Audiobooks (Scholastic, 2000).

Companies That Sell Audiobooks

Agency for Instructional Technology
P.O. Box 1397
1800 N. Stonelake Drive
Bloomington, IN 47404
1-800-457-4509
www.ait.net

Society for Visual Education
6677 North Northwest Highway
Chicago, IL 60631-1304
1-800-829-1900
www.svemedia.com

Blackboard Entertainment
2647 International Blvd., Suite 853
Oakland, CA 94601
1-800-968-2261
www.blackboardkids.com

Recorded Books
270 Skipjack Road
Prince Frederick, MD 20678
1-800-638-1304
www.recordedbooks.com

Audio Bookshelf
174 Prescott Hill Road
Northport, ME 04849
1-800-234-1713

The Learning Company, Inc.
6493 Kaiser Drive
Fremont, CA 94555
1-510-792-2101
www.learningco.com

Listening Library
One Park Avenue
Old Greenwich, CT 06870
1-800-243-4504

Books on Tape
P.O. Box 7900
Newport Beach, CA 92658
1-800-626-3333

BDD Audio
1540 Broadway
New York, NY 10036
1-800-223-6834

DK Multimedia
95 Madison Avenue
New York, NY 10016
1-800-356-6575
www.dk.com

Spoken Arts
8 Lawn Avenue
P.O. Box 100
New Rochelle, NY 10802

Harper Audio
10 E. 53rd St.
New York, NY 10022
1-800-242-7737

Weston Woods
12 Oakwood Avenue
Norwalk, CT 06850-1318
1-800-243-5020
www.scholastic.com

READ 180 Audiobooks
Scholastic Inc.
557 Broadway
New York, NY 10012
1-800-724-6527
www.scholastic.com

Building Fluency Scholastic Professional Books

Lesson 4

Activities to Model Intonation (Using Punctuation)

To teach appropriate intonation while reading, make students aware of the importance of using punctuation as a guide.

Use the following activities:

1. Recite the alphabet or numbers as a conversation. For example,
ABC? DE. FGH! I? JKL. MN? OPQ! RST! UV? WX. YZ!
123. 4! 567? 89. 10!

2. Recite a sentence using different end punctuation.
Cows moo. Cows moo? Cows moo!
Dogs bark? Dogs bark. Dogs bark!

3. Practice placing the stress on different words in a sentence.
I am sad. I *am* sad. I am *sad*.
We are happy. We *are* happy. We are *happy*.

4. Practice reading sentences as if talking to a friend. Have students record their readings, play them back, and evaluate them with a partner or teacher.

Many books provide excellent practice reading text with the correct intonation. *Oink* and *Oink Oink*, both by Arthur Geisert (Houghton Mifflin, 1991 and 1993), offer an engaging way for students to demonstrate correct intonation when reading.

Building Fluency Scholastic Professional Books

Lesson 5

Activities to Model Phrasing (Using Prepositions)

Make students aware that their knowledge of grammar will help them appropriately chunk text as they read. For example, if students can readily identify prepositions, they can more easily chunk text that contains prepositional phrases.

Use the following activities:

1. Provide students with passages in which the prepositional phrases are underlined or highlighted. Explain that a prepositional phrase is a chunk of text that they can use as a guide to phrasing. Model the skill for students.

Sample Passage

She quickly went <u>up to the front room</u>. <u>Of course</u>, <u>by then</u>, Jack was already running <u>out the front door</u>. When he saw Lucy come after him, he laughed and dashed <u>off into the woods</u>. He thought it was all a big game.

2. Distribute a brief preselected passage containing several prepositional phrases. Help students identify each preposition and underline or highlight each prepositional phrase. Have students practice their phrasing skills with a partner using the passage.

Prepositions

about	beneath	excepting	out	under
above	beside	for	outside	underneath
across	besides	from	over	until
after	between	in	past	up
against	beyond	inside	regarding	upon
along	but	into	round	with
among	by	like	since	within
around	concerning	near	through	without
at	despite	of	throughout	
before	down	off	till	
behind	during	on	to	
below	except	onto	toward	

Prepositional Phrases

according to	because of	in addition to	in spite of	with respect to
along with	by means of	in case of	instead of	with reference to
apart from	by reason of	in front of	on account of	with the exception of
as for	by way of	in lieu of	out of	
as regards	due to	in place of	up to	
as to	except for	in regard to	with regard to	

Building Fluency Scholastic Professional Books

Lesson 6

Activities to Model Phrasing (Using Subject/Predicate)

Make students aware that their knowledge of grammar will help them appropriately chunk text as they read. For example, if students can readily identify the difference between a subject and a predicate, they can more easily chunk text based on these two main parts of a sentence.

Use the following activities:

1. Distribute copies of a short preselected passage with the subject underlined once and the predicate underlined twice. Explain that these two main parts of a sentence are natural chunks of text. Have students use the passage to practice their phrasing skills with a partner.

Sample Passage

Many people were on the job. Some workers picked corn. Others put it in sacks. Then the sacks were put on the back of the llama. The llama walked each sack to the terraces. There, the sacks were placed on a truck.

2. Provide students with a short passage. This can be a page from a selection students will read in the upcoming week. Help them highlight or underline the subject or predicate in each sentence. Model how to use these phrase chunks to read fluently.

Lesson 7

Activity to Model Phrasing* (Using Conjunctions)

Make students aware that their knowledge of grammar (in this case conjunctions) will help them appropriately chunk text as they read. Explain that conjunctions signal natural breaks in text that can help the reader phrase appropriately.

Use the following activity:

- Distribute copies of a short preselected passage in which conjunctions join the parts of a compound sentence. Underline the conjunction. Explain that in these sentences, the conjunctions join two complete phrases, each with a subject and predicate. Model phrasing the sentence using the conjunction as a natural pause. For example, *I rode my bike,/ and I played soccer/ in the park*. Have students use the passage to practice their phrasing skills with a partner.

Sample Passage

The men finally saw the injured mountain lion. After the man from the zoo shot her, the big cat fell to the ground. She landed hard. They put her on a stretcher **and** then they carried her

* Use for grades 4–6 only.

Building Fluency   Scholastic Professional Books

to a truck. When they passed by with the stretcher, I looked down at the cat. Her eyes were rolled back in her head. Her mouth was a little open **and** her tongue was hanging out. Then they put her in the truck **and** they drove away. Things really got busy for me after that. I still don't know why, **but** I felt sad for the lion. I hoped the man from the zoo could help her.

Conjunctions (connects words and word groups)

and	for	both—and	not only—but also
but	so	either—or	whether—or
or	yet	neither—nor	
nor			

Subordinating Conjunctions (marks a dependent clause; connects it with a main clause)

after	before	though	whenever
although	if	till	where
as	once	unless	wherever
as if	since	until	while
because	that	when	with the exception of

Lesson 8

Oral Reading Modeling

Explain to students that in order to be fluent readers, they need to pay attention to and practice the traits of skilled readers. These include reading at the correct speed, reading the words in a text with ease, and raising and lowering your voice appropriately when reading.

Use the following activity:

1. Select a short story or passage and read it aloud expressively. Discuss the selection. Create and record a class summary. Discuss elements of the text related to phrasing and intonation.

These elements may include the following:

* reading dialogue as if it is spoken

* the difference between statement, exclamation, and question voices

* reading longer sentences with appropriate pauses

2. Then, allow students to practice reading sections of the story, both on their own and with your help. Have students select a section of the story to read aloud to the class. Monitor their phrasing, intonation, rate, and accuracy. You may wish to record their readings.

Building Fluency Scholastic Professional Books

Sample Passage, Grade 2

A House for Bird
by Ann Dickson

Bird said, "I want a new house."
"This is too little!"
"Let's go look," said Snail.

Bird and Snail went along.
They went up and went down.
They went here and went there.
Was there a new house for Bird?

Is this a house? No, not this.
Is that a house? No, not that.
Snail said, "I see something!"
"Could it be a house for Bird?"

A shoe for a house?
First, Bird swept it out.
Next, Snail scrubbed it off.
Then, they polished it all over.

Snail said, "Go on in, Bird."
"See how you like it."
Bird said, "You come in, too."
"I am in my house," said Snail.

"I love it!" said Bird.
"This house is good for me."
"Yes, but soon this house could be
too little, too," Snail said.

© 2000 by Scholastic Inc.

> "Read dialogue as if it is spoken."

> "Raise your voice at the end of a question sentence. Read an exclamation sentence with excitement."

> "Break up longer sentences into meaningful chunks."

A House for Bird

Bird wanted a new house because hers was too small. She went with her friend Snail to find a house. They found an empty shoe. Bird cleaned it, fixed it up, and moved in.

Lesson 9

Repeated Readings

Repeated readings have been shown to increase reading rate and accuracy. Students transfer the skills they acquire to other texts.

Provide each student with a selection on his or her reading level. Use your copy to mark the student's errors. Follow this routine:

1. Time the student reading for one minute. Mark the stopping point on your copy of the selection.

2. Provide feedback to the student on the number of words he or she read correctly per minute and discuss word recognition errors.

3. Record, on a chart (graph), the words the student read correctly per minute. (See sample chart above and blank chart, opposite, that you can copy and use.)

4. Have students practice reading their selection independently or with a partner.

5. Time the student again. Students may wish to continue reading until they reach a words-per-minute goal they have established for themselves.

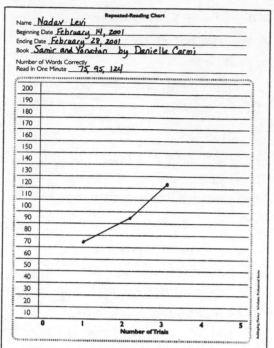

To motivate repeated readings, have students read to a child in a lower grade, tape-record their readings, or prepare a Reader's Theater version of the selection.

Lesson 10

Time-on-Task Reading Boosters (Round-Robin Reading Alternatives)

Round-robin reading is not the most effective way to develop fluency. Students need to read entire selections. Some alternatives to round-robin reading include the following:

∗ Have students read the story silently a few pages at a time, then question them about their reading.

∗ Circulate and listen in as students read softly to themselves.

∗ Call on students frequently and randomly, often in the middle of a paragraph, to read aloud.

If you use round-robin reading, have students read the entire selection independently or with a partner following the group reading.

Building Fluency Scholastic Professional Books

Repeated-Reading Chart

Name _____

Beginning Date _____

Ending Date _____

Book _____

Number of Words Correctly
Read in One Minute _____

200					
190					
180					
170					
160					
150					
140					
130					
120					
110					
100					
90					
80					
70					
60					
50					
40					
30					
20					
10					
0	**1**	**2**	**3**	**4**	**5**

Number of Trials

Lesson 11

Speed Drills

Speed drills build fluency because they help students rapidly recognize common syllables and spelling patterns in multisyllabic words. And they're fun!

You can use the speed-drill reproducibles (pages 57–67), which include examples of all the spelling patterns as well as high-frequency words. And you can create your own drills using the blank 50- and 100-word charts (pages 55 and 56). To gather words for your drills, draw on the word lists that begin on page 75.

1. Distribute copies of the speed drill to students. Allow students two minutes to underline the target syllable or spelling pattern. For example, if the skill is words ending in consonant +*le*, have students underline *ble*, *cle*, and *ple* in any words containing these common patterns. If the skill is to recognize vowel teams, have them underline those letters.

2. When finished, have students use their speed-drill sheet to read the marked words. Help students pronounce the common syllables or spelling patterns.

3. As an incentive, students may record their speed-drill scores on a chart (page 54). Have

Building Fluency Scholastic Professional Books

them record the score for each testing of the speed drill. Work with each student to set individual speed-drill goals—a set number of words to read in a minute, for example.

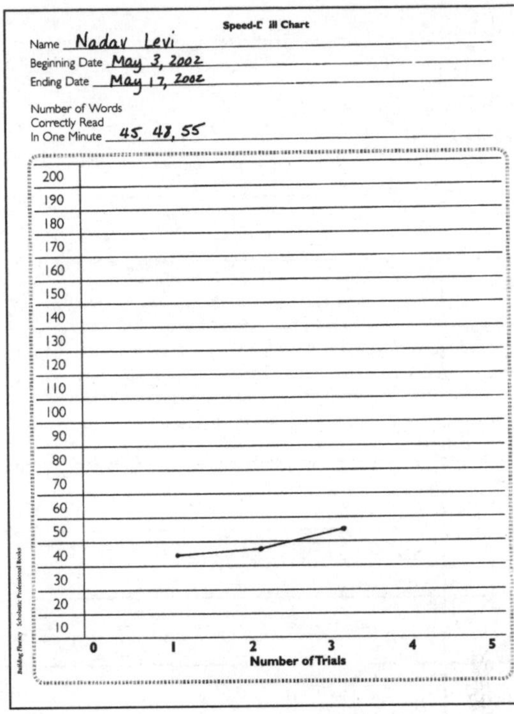

Speed drills should cover the following six common syllable spelling patterns:

1. closed: These syllables end in a consonant. The vowel sound is generally short (examples: _rab_bit, _nap_kin).

2. open: These syllables end in a vowel. The vowel sound is generally long (examples: _ti_ger, _pi_lot).

3. vowel-silent _e_: These syllables generally represent long-vowel sounds (examples: com_pete_, de_cide_).

4. vowel team: Many vowel sounds are spelled with vowel digraphs such as _ai, ay, ea, ee, oa, ow, oo, oi, oy, ou, ie,_ and _ei._ The vowel digraphs, or teams, appear in the same syllable (examples: b_oa_t, expl_ai_n).

5. r-controlled: When a vowel is followed by _r_, the letter _r_ affects the sound of the vowel. The vowel and the _r_ appear in the same syllable (examples: b_ir_d, t_ur_tle).

6. consonant + _le_: Usually when _le_ appears at the end of a word and is preceded by a consonant, the consonant + _le_ form the final syllable (examples: ta_ble_, lit_tle_).

The chart in the margin shows:

Name __Nadav Levi__
Beginning Date __May 3, 2002__
Ending Date __May 17, 2002__

Number of Words
Correctly Read
In One Minute __45, 48, 55__

Put It Into Practice!

Tips for Creating Speed Drills

✓ Select skills with which your students need to develop automaticity (i.e., words containing a specific phonics skill or irregular high-frequency words).

✓ Select either a 50-word or 100-word Speed-Drill form based on the age of your students. I suggest using the 50-word drills for younger students or for newly-learned skills.

✓ Select 20–25 words to include on the speed drill. Write the words in random order, multiple times, on the speed-drill form. Make copies of the speed drill for students to use. (Note: For some skills, you may not want to repeat any of the words or syllables, especially if the speed drill covers review skills or multiple skills.)

✓ Allow students time to practice reading the words on the speed drills independently. Suggest that they underline or highlight the target skill. For example, have students underline _ee_ and _ea_ in all the long _e_ words.

Speed-Drill Chart

Name _____

Beginning Date _____

Ending Date _____

Number of Words
Correctly Read
In One Minute _____

200					
190					
180					
170					
160					
150					
140					
130					
120					
110					
100					
90					
80					
70					
60					
50					
40					
30					
20					
10					
	0	1	2	3	4	5

Number of Trials

Name _____ Date _____

50-Word Speed Drill

Name _____ Date_____

100-Word Speed Drill

Name _____ Date _____

Closed-Syllable Speed Drill

Underline the first syllable in each word. This is a closed syllable, which ends in a consonant and has the short vowel sound. Then practice reading the words until you are ready to be timed.

admit	basket	cabin	comet	contact
custom	dentist	exit	fidget	fossil
goblin	habit	hidden	kitten	limit
magnet	mental	mitten	picnic	problem
plastic	publish	pumpkin	random	ribbon
rotten	sadden	satin	signal	sunset
tablet	tennis	tonsil	tunnel	upset
victim	vivid	welcome	witness	zigzag
budget	chicken	jogger	figment	muffin
practice	puppet	crimson	denim	nostril

Open-Syllable Speed Drill

Underline the open syllable in each word. The open syllable ends in a vowel and has the long vowel sound. Then practice reading the words until you are ready to be timed.

baby	bacon	basic	bison	bonus
cedar	cider	cobra	cozy	cradle
crisis	decent	diver	donut	even
fatal	female	focus	frequent	frozen
global	gravy	human	item	label
lady	lazy	lilac	major	minus
moment	music	naval	open	pilot
polo	prefix	program	pupil	rebate
recent	rodent	silent	slogan	table
tidal	tiger	vacant	virus	vocal

Final (silent) –e Syllable Speed Drill

Practice reading the words until you are ready to be timed.

bit	bite	can	cane	cap
cape	cod	code	cub	cube
cut	cute	dim	dime	fad
fade	fat	fate	fin	fine
glob	globe	grad	grade	hat
hate	hid	hide	hop	hope
kit	kite	mad	made	not
note	past	paste	pin	pine
plan	plane	rid	ride	rob
robe	scrap	scrape	slid	slide

Name _____ Date_____

Final (silent) –e Syllable Speed Drill

Underline the final–*e* syllable in each word. The final–*e* syllable has the long vowel sound.
Then practice reading the words until you are ready to be timed.

bake	advice	blame	athlete	cage
confuse	daze	complete	fame	collide
page	delete	place	describe	scrape
female	slide	excite	bike	erase
twice	humane	broke	incline	bone
remote	smoke	profile	slope	notebook
use	reptile	cute	sincere	eve
mistake	nose	translate	smile	tadpole
whale	donate	white	animate	stake
demonstrate	price	estimate	life	coincide

Vowel-Team Syllable Speed Drill

Underline the vowel team in each word. The vowel team appears in the same syllable. Then practice reading the words until you are ready to be timed. Note: Some vowel teams contain a consonant acting as a vowel (for example _ow_ in _cow_ or _ay_ in _play_).

abound	yellow	about	withdraw	account
window	agree	volunteer	allow	viewpoint
amount	unreal	appear	unclear	appoint
turmoil	approach	trainer	away	textbook
balloon	subway	canteen	seesaw	complain
reveal	chimney	repeat	cuckoo	employ
enjoy	raincoat	exclaim	fellow	holiday
proceed	pillow	halfway	midweek	monkey
obtain	essay	cartoon	classroom	compound
poison	railroad	raccoon	Sunday	release

r-Controlled Vowel Syllable Speed Drill

Underline the vowel plus *r* in each word. The vowel plus *r* appears in the same syllable. Then practice reading the words until you are ready to be timed.

slipper	murmur	glimmer	comfort	slender
mortal	color	morning	gerbil	clutter
clover	garnish	monster	skipper	sister
garden	mister	circus	garlic	modern
chorus	winter	silver	galore	whisker
charter	merchant	turtle	further	merit
chapter	forty	servant	vertical	formal
center	finger	margin	scarlet	vapor
carton	expert	liver	litter	tractor
guitar	cursor	stardom	invert	labor

Name _____ Date_____

Consonant + *le* Syllable Speed Drill

Practice reading the syllables until you are ready to be timed.

ble	cle	dle	fle	gle
cle	zle	kle	tle	ple
fle	ble	gle	cle	ple
zle	gle	fle	kle	dle
cle	zle	ble	ple	dle
tle	zle	ble	tle	kle
cle	dle	tle	zle	ple
fle	cle	dle	ble	gle
zle	fle	cle	gle	ple
dle	ble	tle	cle	zle

Name _____ Date_____

Consonant + *le* Syllable Speed Drill

Underline the consonant + *le* in each word. (The consonant + *le* appears in the same syllable.)
Then practice reading the words until you are ready to be timed.

bubble	battle	angle	bridle	apple
ankle	double	bottle	bugle	bundle
circle	crinkle	fable	cattle	eagle
fiddle	maple	dazzle	marble	gentle
giggle	handle	purple	fizzle	noble
kettle	jungle	kindle	sample	muzzle
pebble	little	shingle	middle	simple
puzzle	rumble	mantle	single	needle
steeple	sparkle	stubble	rattle	struggle
puddle	temple	sprinkle	tumble	settle
wiggle	puddle	uncle	wrinkle	title
saddle	vehicle	bubble	double	battle
fable	bottle	angle	title	cattle
eagle	circle	fiddle	bundle	handle
middle	steeple	marble	apple	gentle
rumble	giggle	tumble	maple	kettle
sample	rattle	needle	uncle	pebble
vehicle	purple	jungle	little	bridle
simple	settle	saddle	single	struggle
ankle	stubble	puzzle	wrinkle	wiggle

High-Frequency Syllable Speed Drill

Practice reading the syllables until you are ready to be timed.

ing	er	ter	tion	re
ver	ex	bout	com	ple
un	der	num	ble	ment
ture	est	dis	im	fi
ture	ing	ment	er	bout
un	ter	com	est	der
ex	dis	ver	ple	re
ble	im	tion	num	fi
dis	un	ing	ple	ble
er	num	est	ter	ture
com	ver	bout	re	der
em	ex	tion	ment	fi
un	er	der	dis	ing
bout	ter	ture	ment	est
im	ble	ex	num	com
tion	re	ver	fi	ple
ter	ble	er	re	un
ing	fi	dis	der	num
ment	tion	ple	est	ver
ture	com	ex	bout	im

Name _____ Date_____

50-Word, High-Frequency Word Speed Drill

Practice reading the words until you are ready to be timed.

the	he	be	what	there
of	for	this	all	said
and	was	from	were	if
to	on	have	when	do
in	are	or	we	will
is	as	by	there	each
you	with	one	can	about
that	his	had	an	how
it	they	not	your	up
a	at	but	which	out

50-Word, High-Frequency Word Speed Drill

100-Word, High-Frequency Word Speed Drill

Practice reading the words until you are ready to be timed.*

that	the	them	there	then
where	when	what	we	who
what	that	them	then	the
where	there	who	when	we
where	them	that	the	when
who	there	we	then	what
who	when	there	that	the
where	we	them	what	then
the	we	what	there	that
where	then	when	them	who
when	then	we	the	there
that	them	who	what	where
there	where	then	them	when
who	that	what	we	the
who	them	there	what	where
then	the	that	we	when
what	who	them	then	the
where	there	when	that	we
them	the	we	where	there
when	what	then	who	that

100-Word, High-Frequency Word Speed Drill

* Students have difficulties distinguishing words that begin with *wh* and *th*. This drill focuses on these words.

Lesson 12

Oral-Reading Fluency Check-Ups

Check students' oral-reading rate at least every 6–8 weeks. Use the following procedure:

1. Make a copy of a test passage for the student and one for yourself, so that you can record the student's errors while he or she is reading.

2. As the student reads, mark any errors on your copy.

3. Use the guidelines provided on page 11. For example, if the student stops or struggles with the word for 3 seconds, tell the student the word and mark it as incorrect.

4. Place a mark after the last word the student reads.

5. Tally the results. Use the norm-referenced charts on page 11 to determine the student's reading rate. Based on the results, establish fluency goals for the student.

Tips for Choosing Reading Passages

✓ Use the San Diego Quick Assessment on the next page to get an approximate grade-level designation for each student. Then, consult a list of published grade-appropriate books. Choose one book on each grade level to use for testing.

✓ Use the phrase-cued, grade-specific passages on pages 27–40.

✓ Select a 100-word passage from the beginning, middle, and end of your basal reading series.

The San Diego Quick Assessment

Preparing the Test

1. Type each list on a note card. Write the grade level on the back for reference.

2. Prepare a typed word list with spaces after each word to record the student's responses.

Administering the Test

1. Have the student read aloud each word from a card at least two years below her grade. If she misses any words, go to easier lists until she makes no errors. This is her base reading level.

2. Have the student read each subsequent card in sequence. Record incorrect responses. Be sure to have the student read *every* word so you can determine her decoding strategies.

3. Continue the assessment until the student misses at least three words on one of the lists.

Scoring the Test

Use the assessment results to identify the student's independent (no more than one error on a list), instructional (two errors on a list), and frustration (three or more errors) levels. Provide instructional and independent reading materials for each child accordingly.

Building Fluency Scholastic Professional Books

Name _____ Date_____

San Diego Quick Assessment

Preprimer	**Primer**	**Grade 1**
see	you	road
play	come	live
me	not	thank
at	with	when
run	jump	bigger
go	help	how
and	is	always
look	work	night
can	are	spring
here	this	today

Grade 2	**Grade 3**	**Grade 4**
our	city	decided
please	middle	served
myself	moment	amazed
town	frightened	silent
early	exclaimed	wrecked
send	several	improved
wide	lonely	certainly
believe	drew	entered
quietly	since	realized
carefully	straight	interrupted

Grade 5	**Grade 6**	**Grade 7**
scanty	bridge	amber
business	commercial	dominion
develop	abolish	sundry
considered	trucker	capillary
discussed	apparatus	impetuous
behaved	elementary	blight
splendid	comment	wrest
acquainted	necessity	enumerate
escaped	gallery	daunted
grim	relativity	condescend

Grade 8	**Grade 9**	**Grade 10**
capacious	conscientious	zany
limitation	isolation	jerkin
pretext	molecule	nausea
intrigue	ritual	gratuitous
delusion	momentous	linear
immaculate	vulnerable	inept
ascent	kinship	legality
acrid	conservatism	aspen
binocular	jaunty	amnesty
embankment	inventive	barometer

LaPray and Ross, 1969

Fluency: The Next Generation

The next wave of researchers are expanding their definition of fluency and exploring the effect of automaticity in areas such as performing phonemic awareness tasks, recognizing the letters of the alphabet, stating common sound-spellings, and identifying high-utility sight words. They are discovering that it is not just a student's accuracy in recognizing letters and words, or performing phonemic-awareness tasks that count in terms of the child's reading progress. It is the speed with which a child can perform these tasks that is critical and telling.

If you are teaching the primary grades, the following assessments can help you check your students' reading fluency.

Phonemic Awareness: Researchers at the University of Oregon are leading the way in developing assessments to test the accuracy and speed with which children can perform such phonemic-awareness tasks as sound matching and oral segmentation. For more information on these assessments, see http://dibels.uoregon.edu/.

Alphabet Recognition: Display the Alphabet Recognition Test on page 71. Ask the student to say the letter names as quickly as possible and time him. Slow, labored identification is common among children who will struggle at learning to read. These children will need a great deal of practice with recognizing and writing the letters in and out of order.

A good follow-up to this test is to have children name the sound that each letter stands for.

Phonics: Use the Nonsense-Word Test on page 73 to assess students' phonics skills. This assessment is NOT recommended for children in Grade 1. The concept of nonsense words may confuse them. However, nonsense words work well for older children because reading them requires the child to use his or her knowledge of sound-spellings to decode each word. There's no chance that the child recognizes the word by sight.

Sight Words: To develop fluency, children must be able to recognize the most common words in written English automatically. You can use The Sight-Word Proficiency and Automaticity Test on page 74 to assess each child's automaticity. Remember, it is not just accuracy, but speed that must be monitored.

If available, use the TOWRE (Test of Word Reading Efficiency) in place of The Sight-Word Test. The TOWRE is a nationally-normed test available from PRO-ED. The address is: PRO-ED, 8700 Shoal Creek Blvd., Austin, TX 78757-6897. Tel: (800) 897-3202.

Building Fluency Scholastic Professional Books

Name _____ Date _____

Alphabet Recognition Test

G	N	E	C	P
S	A	K	O	J
D	I	W	F	V
Z	T	B	R	H
L	Q	U	M	Y

s	m	g	y	p
b	w	q	k	h
r	d	a	x	z
o	j	t	l	c
f	n	i	e	u

The Nonsense-Word Test

Preparing the Test

1. Type or print the test on a sheet of paper.

2. Prepare an answer sheet for you to record the student's responses.

Administering the Test

1. Administer the test to one student at a time.

2. Explain to the student that he or she is to read each word. Point out that the words are nonsense, or made-up, words.

3. Have the student read the entire list.

4. Write a check mark on the answer sheet for each word read correctly.

Scoring the Test

1. Count a word correct if the pronunciation is correct according to common sound-spelling relationships.

2. Total the number of words read correctly. Analyze the mispronounced words, looking for patterns that might give you information about the student's decoding strengths and weaknesses.

3. Focus future instruction on those sound-spelling relationship categories (short vowels, long vowels, etc.) in which the student made three or more errors.

The Sight-Word Profiency and Automaticity Test (page 74)

Preparing the Test

1. Type or print the test on a sheet of paper.

2. Prepare an answer sheet for you to record the student's responses.

Administering the Test

1. Administer the test to one student at a time.

2. For The Sight-Word Proficiency and Automaticity Test, explain to the student that he or she is to read each word as quickly as possible.

3. Have the student read as many words as possible within 90 seconds. Use a stopwatch or other timer to time the student.

4. Write a check mark on the answer sheet for each word read incorrectly or skipped.

Scoring the Test

1. Count the words read correctly in 90 seconds.

2. Total the number of words read correctly. Analyze the mispronounced words, looking for patterns that might give you information about the student's decoding strengths and weaknesses.

3. Provide additional instruction on words students read incorrectly or omit. Retest students every six weeks and monitor progress.

The Nonsense-Word Test

A. Short Vowels

1. lat
2. ped
3. sib
4. mog
5. vun
6. fim
7. hep
8. yot
9. rud
10. cag

B. Digraphs, Blends

1. sheg
2. chab
3. stot
4. whid
5. thuzz
6. bruck
7. cliss
8. smend
9. thrist
10. phum

C. Long Vowels

1. sote
2. mabe
3. foap
4. weam
5. flay
6. shain
7. dright
8. hupe
9. heest
10. sny

D. Other Vowels

1. doit
2. spoud
3. clar
4. foy
5. jern
6. moof
7. lurst
8. porth
9. stook
10. flirch

E. Multisyllabic Words

1. rigfap
2. churbit
3. napsate
4. reatloid
5. foutray
6. moku
7. wolide
8. lofam
9. pagbo
10. plizzle

Name _____ Date_____

The Sight-Word Proficiency and Automaticity Test

the	into	also	will	go
of	has	around	each	good
and	more	another	about	new
a	her	came	how	write
to	two	come	up	our
in	like	work	out	used
is	him	three	them	me
you	see	word	then	man
that	time	must	she	too
it	could	because	many	any
he	no	does	some	day
for	make	part	so	same
was	than	even	these	right
on	first	place	would	look
are	been	well	other	think
but	long	as	its	such
what	little	with	who	here
all	very	his	now	take
were	after	they	people	why
when	words	at	my	things
we	called	be	made	help
there	just	this	over	put
can	where	from	did	years
an	most	I	down	different
your	know	have	only	away
which	get	or	way	again
their	through	by	find	off
said	back	one	use	went
if	much	had	may	old
do	before	not	water	number

Speed-Drill Word Lists

Closed-Syllable Syllabication Pattern

absent
active
admit
album
anklet
antic
atlas
attic
axis
basket
beggar
beverage
blanket
blister
bobbin
bonnet
budget
button
cabin
cactus
campus
cancer
candid
cannot
canvas
canyon
catnap
catnip
channel
chicken
cluster
comet
comic
common
contact
content
contest
context
cosmic
cottage
cotton
crimson
culprit
custom
cutlet
dapple
denim
dental
dentist
dismal
distant
dollar
eggnog
engine
exit
fabric
falcon
fasten
fatten
fender
fidget
figment
filter
fossil

frantic
gallon
goblet
goblin
gospel
gossip
habit
hangar
hatbox
hectic
helmet
hiccup
hidden
hostel
husband
index
inlet
insect
instinct
insult
jacket
jogger
kingdom
kitchen
kitten
lesson
limit
litmus
madcap
magnet
manner
mantel
mascot
mental
metric
midget
mishap
mitten
muffin
napkin
nectar
nostril
padlock
panic
pasture
pencil
picnic
picture
pigment
plaster
plastic
plumber
pocket
pollen
practice
pregnant
pretzel
princess
problem
public
publish
pumpkin
puppet
rabbit
random
ransom
rapid

ribbon
robin
rotten
rustic
sadden
sandwich
satin
septic
signal
socket
splendor
splinter
subject
submit
sudden
suffix
summit
sunset
suntan
sunup
suspect
tablet
tactic
tandem
tantrum
tendon
tennis
ticket
tidbit
timid
tonsil
tractor
transit
tremor
tunnel
until
upset
valid
velvet
victim
vivid
vulture
welcome
witness
zigzag

Open-Syllable Syllabication Pattern

agent
baby
bacon
bagel
basal
basic
basin
basis
biceps
bison
blatant
bogus
bonus
butane
cedar
cider
cobalt

cobra
cogent
colon
cozy
cradle
crazy
crisis
cubic
cupid
data
decent
demon
depot
diver
donate
donor
donut
edict
ego
equal
even
evil
fatal
favor
feline
female
final
finite
focal
focus
fragrant
frequent
frozen
future
global
gracious
gravy
grocery
halo
helix
hijack
holy
human
humid
idol
irate
iris
item
label
lady
latent
latex
lazy
legal
lethal
lilac
local
locate
locust
major
migraine
minus
mogul
moment
motor
mucus
museum

music
mutate
nasal
nature
naval
navy
obese
odor
open
oval
ozone
penal
phony
photo
pilot
pliers
polo
pony
prefix
primate
probate
profile
program
propane
pupil
raven
rebate
recent
regal
rhino
rival
rodent
saber
sacred
secret
senile
sequence
sequin
silent
silo
sinus
siren
slogan
social
solo
spinal
spiral
stamen
table
tidal
tidy
tiger
tirade
titan
token
total
totem
tribal
unit
vacant
vagrant
vinyl
virus
vital
vocal
yo-yo
zebra

Final-e (VCe) Syllabication Pattern

abuse
accuse
advice
advise
aflame
alone
alpine
amaze
amuse
animate
anyplace
appetite
arcade
athlete
awake
backbone
bathrobe
bedtime
birthplace
blockade
boneless
bookcase
calcite
captivate
calculate
candidate
capsize
cascade
celebrate
cheesecake
classmate
coincide
collide
combine
commode
commune
compare
compete
compile
complete
concise
concrete
confuse
connote
console
contemplate
convene
crusade
cupcake
cyclone
daytime
debate
deflate
degrade
delete
demonstrate
describe
desire
despite
dethrone
device
devote
dictate
diffuse

disclose
disgrace
dislike
dispute
divine
donate
drainpipe
efface
eliminate
empire
enclose
engage
entice
episode
erase
erode
escape
estate
estimate
evaluate
exchange
excite
excuse
exhale
explode
explore
expose
extreme
fanfare
feline
female
finely
finite
fireplace
franchise
fructose
frustrate
galore
gateway
graphite
handmade
handshake
headline
hesitate
homemade
hopeless
ignite
illustrate
imbibe
immune
impede
impose
incite
incline
inflate
inhale
innate
insane
inside
insulate
intimidate
invade
keepsake
landscape
lateness
lemonade
lifeboat

Speed-Drill Word Lists (cont.)

locate
lonesome
maypole
mealtime
membrane
microscope
microwave
mistake
negate
nickname
nightingale
nineteen
ninety
notebook
obscene
octane
offstage
oppose
outrage
overcame
overtake
ozone
pancake
parade
persuade
phoneme
pipeline
pomade
porcupine
prepare
profane
profile
propose
provide
rattlesnake
rebate
rebuke
recede
recite
refine
refuse
regulate
relate
remote
replete
reptile
retire
sacrifice
sapphire
secrete
severe
shameful
shoelace
sidewalk
sincere
snowflake
stampede
sublime
subscribe
subside
summertime
tailgate
teenage
telephone
textile
translate
trombone

unmade
upgrade
upscale
wasteland
whaleboat
widespread
wildlife
xylophone

One-Syllable VCe

long a
ace
age
bake
base
blade
blame
blaze
brace
brake
brave
cage
cake
came
cane
cape
case
cave
chase
crane
crate
date
daze
drape
face
fade
fake
fame
flake
flame
frame
game
gate
gave
gaze
glaze
grace
grade
grape
grate
grave
haste
hate
haze
jade
lace
lake
lame
lane
late
made
make
male
mane
mate

name
pace
page
pale
pane
paste
pave
place
plane
plate
quake
race
rage
rake
rate
rave
safe
sake
sale
same
save
scale
scrape
shade
shake
shame
shape
shave
skate
slate
snake
space
spade
stage
stake
stale
state
take
tale
tame
tape
taste
trace
trade
vane
vase
wade
wage
wake
wave
waste
whale

long i
bike
bite
bride
chime
crime
dice
dime
dine
dive
drive
file
fine
five

glide
hide
hike
hive
kite
lice
life
like
lime
line
live
mice
mile
mine
nice
nine
pile
pine
pipe
price
pride
rice
ride
ripe
rise
shine
side
slice
slide
slime
smile
spice
spike
spine
stride
strike
stripe
swine
tide
tile
time
twice
twine
vine
while
white
wide
wife
wipe
wise
write

long o
bone
broke
choke
chose
close
code
cone
dome
drove
globe
hole
home
hope
hose

joke
lone
mole
nose
note
poke
pole
robe
rode
rope
rose
slope
smoke
spoke
stole
stone
stove
stroke
those
tone
vote
whole
woke
zone

long u
cube
cute
fuse
mule
use

Vowel-Team Syllabication Pattern
abound
about
account
affair
agree
agreed
airfare
allow
aloud
amount
annoy
appeal
appear
appoint
approach
assault
away
baboon
ballgown
balloon
beneath
blackmail
canteen
cartoon
chimney
classroom
cocoon
coffee
complain
complaint
compound

contain
convey
cuckoo
decay
devour
discount
display
donkey
dugout
elbow
emcee
employ
enjoy
essay
esteem
exclaim
exhaust
explain
exploit
fellow
fingernail
follow
fourteen
freeload
galley
halfway
handbook
hockey
holiday
impeach
indeed
mermaid
midair
midweek
mislead
mistreat
Monday
monkey
moonbeam
mushroom
oatmeal
obtain
overpaid
pedigree
pillow
poison
prevail
proceed
reveal
seesaw
shallow
spoilage
subway
Sunday
tattoo
textbook
thirteen
trainer
turmoil
unafraid
unclear
unfair
unreal
valley
viewpoint
volunteer
window

withdraw
yellow

r-Controlled Vowel Syllabication Pattern
aboard
absorb
adhere
admire
adore
adorn
afford
after
airplane
alarm
anger
appear
ardent
arson
artist
assert
barber
batter
before
berry
better
birthday
blister
blizzard
border
burden
burlap
butter
cancer
carbon
carton
cashmere
cellar
center
certify
certain
chairperson
chapter
charcoal
charter
cheerful
cherish
chorus
circus
clover
clutter
color
comfort
concert
confer
consort
copper
courtship
cursor
curtain
dairy
desert
differ
dinner

Speed-Drill Word Lists (cont.)

dirty	lunar	soccer	boggle	joggle	spackle	eternal
discard	manner	solar	bottle	jumble	sparkle	experimental
distort	margin	sordid	bridle	jungle	spindle	external
disturb	market	spider	bristle	kettle	sprinkle	feudal
doctor	marshal	splinter	brittle	kindle	squabble	focal
dollar	master	spurious	bubble	knuckle	squiggle	fraternal
dormant	matter	stairway	buckle	little	steeple	fundamental
dreary	member	stardom	bugle	mantle	straddle	global
duration	merchant	sterling	bundle	maple	stumble	hospital
earache	merit	suburb	bungle	marble	swashbuckle	illegal
earliest	merriment	summer	cable	meddle	swindle	incidental
effort	mister	supper	cackle	middle	tabernacle	instrumental
endurance	modern	target	castle	mingle	table	internal
enter	monster	tearful	cattle	muddle	tackle	jackal
entire	morning	temper	chronicle	mumble	tattle	journal
error	mortal	tender	chuckle	muscle	temple	judgmental
expert	murmur	terrace	circle	muzzle	thimble	kernel
explore	nearby	terrible	coddle	needle	thistle	label
fairway	never	thermos	crackle	nibble	throttle	legal
favor	normal	thirsty	crinkle	noble	tickle	local
filter	northwest	thunder	crumble	noodle	timetable	maternal
finger	number	timber	cuddle	nuzzle	tingle	medal
fireman	nurture	torture	curable	ogle	title	mental
flirtatious	offer	tractor	curdle	paddle	toddle	metal
floral	otter	tumor	dawdle	pebble	treble	mislabel
formal	parcel	turkey	dazzle	peddle	tremble	model
fortress	pardon	turnip	debacle	periwinkle	trickle	monumental
forty	pattern	under	diddle	pickle	tricycle	mussel
fourteen	pearly	unstirred	dimple	piddle	triple	nickel
further	peering	urban	disable	pimple	trouble	nocturnal
galore	pepper	urgent	doodle	pinochle	truffle	ornamental
garden	perfect	vapor	double	poodle	tumble	parental
garlic	peril	varnish	dribble	prattle	turtle	paternal
garnish	person	vendor	drizzle	puddle	tussle	pedal
gerbil	plaster	vertical	durable	purple	twiddle	petal
girded	platter	virtue	dwindle	puzzle	twinkle	pumpernickel
glory	portal	whether	eagle	quadruple	unable	rebel
guitar	porthole	whirlwind	enable	quibble	uncle	regal
hairbrush	pouring	whisker	fable	ramshackle	unstable	rental
hammer	prairie	winter	fickle	rattle	vehicle	sentimental
harness	purchase	yearling	fiddle	resemble	waddle	shrivel
harvest	razor		fizzle	riddle	whistle	snivel
herald	rebirth		freckle	ripple	whittle	strudel
herbal	rehearse	**Words with -le, -al, -el Syllabication Pattern: Speed-Drill Word List**	fumble	rubble	wiggle	swivel
hereby	resource		gentle	rumble	wobble	temperamental
hermit	restore		giggle	rustle	wrinkle	transcendental
hoarding	return		girdle	sable		transmittal
hopper	revere		gobble	saddle		vocal
hornet	rubber		goggle	sample	**Consonant + al or el Words**	yokel
hunger	rumor	**Consonant + le words**	grapple	scramble		
ignore	scarlet		griddle	scribble	accidental	
immerse	scatter	able	gristle	scruple	acquittal	
import	scoreless	angle	grumble	scuffle	bifocal	
infer	searchlight	ankle	guzzle	scuttle	brutal	
inspire	servant	apple	handle	Seattle	chapel	
invert	severe	Aristotle	heckle	securable	chisel	
jargon	shelter	assemble	hobble	settle	coincidental	
kernel	sheriff	babble	honeysuckle	shackle	committal	
labor	silver	battle	huddle	shingle	conical	
ladder	sincere	bauble	humble	shuffle	continental	
lantern	sister	beagle	hurdle	shuttle	cymbal	
laser	skipper	beetle	hurtle	sickle	dental	
lemur	skirmish	befuddle	hustle	simple	detrimental	
letter	slender	belittle	icicle	single	dismissal	
litter	slipper	bible	incurable	sizzle	drivel	
liver	snorkel	bicycle	jiggle	skedaddle	duffel	
lumber	soared	bobble	jingle	snuffle	environmental	

Lists of High-Frequency Syllables and Words

102 Most Common Non-Word Syllables

ing	tain
er	ning
i	col
y	par
ter	dis
al	ern
ed	ny
es	cit
e	po
tion	cal
re	mu
o	moth
oth	pic
ry	im
de	coun
ver	mon
ex	pe
en	lar
di	por
bout	fi
com	bers
ple	sec
u	ap
con	stud
per	ad
un	tween
der	gan
tle	bod
ber	tence
ty	ward
num	hap
peo	nev
ble	ure
af	mem
ers	ters
mer	cov
wa	ger
ment	nit
pro	
ar	
ma	
ri	
sen	
ture	
fer	
dif	
pa	
tions	
ther	
fore	
est	
fa	
la	
el	
n't	
si	
ent	
ven	
ev	
ac	
ca	
fol	
ful	
na	

322 Most Frequent Syllables in the 5,000 Most Frequent English Words

1. ing
2. er
3. a
4. ly
5. ed
6. i
7. es
8. re
9. tion
10. in
11. e
12. con
13. y
14. ter
15. ex
16. al
17. de
18. com
19. o
20. di
21. en
22. an
23. ty
24. ry
25. u
26. ti
27. ri
28. be
29. per
30. to
31. pro
32. ac
33. ad
34. ar
35. ers
36. ment
37. or
38. tions
39. ble
40. der
41. ma
42. na
43. si
44. un
45. at
46. dis
47. ca
48. cal
49. man
50. ap
51. po
52. sion
53. vi
54. el
55. est
56. la
57. lar
58. pa
59. ture
60. for
61. is
62. mer
63. pe
64. ra
65. so
66. ta
67. as
68. col
69. fi
70. ful
71. ger
72. low
73. ni
74. par
75. son
76. tle
77. day
78. ny
79. pen
80. pre
81. tive
82. car
83. ci
84. mo
85. on
86. ous
87. pi
88. se
89. ten
90. tor
91. ver
92. ber
93. can
94. dy
95. et
96. it
97. mu
98. no
99. ple
100. cu
101. fac
102. fer
103. gen
104. ic
105. land
106. light
107. ob
108. of
109. pos
110. tain
111. den
112. ings
113. mag
114. ments
115. set
116. some
117. sub
118. sur
119. ters
120. tu
121. af
122. au
123. cy
124. fa
125. im
126. li
127. lo
128. men
129. min
130. mon
131. op
132. out
133. rec
134. ro
135. sen
136. side
137. tal
138. tic
139. ties
140. ward
141. age
142. ba
143. but
144. cit
145. cle
146. co
147. cov
148. da
149. dif
150. ence
151. ern
152. eve
153. hap
154. ies
155. ket
156. lec
157. main
158. mar
159. mis
160. my
161. nal
162. ness
163. ning
164. n't
165. nu
166. oc
167. pres
168. sup
169. te
170. ted
171. tem
172. tin
173. tri
174. tro
175. up
176. va
177. ven
178. vis
179. am
180. bor
181. by
182. cat
183. cent
184. ev
185. gan
186. gle
187. head
188. high
189. il
190. lu
191. me
192. nore
193. part
194. por
195. read
196. rep
197. su
198. tend
199. ther
200. ton
201. try
202. um
203. uer
204. way
205. ate
206. bet
207. bles
208. bod
209. cap
210. cial
211. cir
212. cor
213. coun
214. cus
215. dan
216. dle
217. ef
218. end
219. ent
220. ered
221. fin
222. form
223. go
224. har
225. ish
226. lands
227. let
228. long
229. mat
230. meas
231. mem
232. mul
233. ner
234. play
235. ples
236. ply
237. port
238. press
239. sat
240. sec
241. ser
242. south
243. sun
244. the
245. ting
246. tra
247. tures
248. val
249. var
250. vid
251. wil
252. win
253. won
254. work
255. act
256. ag
257. air
258. als
259. bat
260. bi
261. cate
262. cen
263. char
264. come
265. cul
266. ders
267. east
268. fect
269. fish
270. fix
271. gi
272. grand
273. great
274. heav
275. ho
276. hunt
277. ion
278. its
279. jo
280. lat
281. lead
282. lect
283. lent
284. less
285. lin
286. mal
287. mi
288. mil
289. moth
290. near
291. nel
292. net
293. new
294. one
295. point
296. prac
297. ral
298. rect
299. ried
300. round
301. row
302. sa
303. sand
304. self
305. sent
306. ship
307. sim
308. sions
309. sis
310. sons
311. stand
312. sug
313. tel
314. tom
315. tors
316. tract
317. tray
318. us
319. vel
320. west
321. where
322. writ

The Most Frequent Words*

the
of
and
a
to
in
is
you
that
it
he
for
was
on
are
but
what
all
were
when
we
there
can
an
your
which
their
said
if

*This list contains the 150 most frequently used words (in order of frequency) in printed school English according to the American Heritage Word Frequency Book.

Lists of High-Frequency Syllables and Words (cont.)

do
them
and
know
upon
why

into
then
any
laugh
us
will

has
she
are
let
use
wish

more
many
around
light
very
with

her
some
as
like
walk
work

two
so
ask
little
want
would

like
these
at
live
warm
write

him
would
ate
long
was
yellow

see
other
away
look
wash
yes

time
its
be
made
we
you

could
who
because
make
well
your

no
now
been
many

make
people
before
may

than
my
best
me

first
made
better
much

been
over
big
must

long
did
black
my

little
down
blue
myself

very
only
both
never

after
way
bring
new

words
find
brown
no

called
use
but
out

just
may
buy
over

where
water
by
own

most
go
done
pick

know
good
don't
play

get
new
down
please

through
write
draw
pretty

back
our
drink
pull

much
used
eat
put

before
me
eight
ran

also
man
every
read

around
too
fall
red

another
any
far
ride

came
day
fast
right

come
same
find
round

work
right
first
run

three
look
five
said

word
think
fly
saw

must
such
for
say

because
here
found
see

does
take
four
seven

part
why
from
shall

even
things
full
she

place
help
funny
show

well
put
gave
sing

as
years
get
sit

with
different
give
six

his
away
go
sleep

they
again
goes
small

at
off
going
so

be
went
good
some

this
old
got
soon

from
number
green
these

I
grow
they

have
had
think

or
Dolch Basic
I
this

by
Sight
if
those

one
Vocabulary 220
in
three

had
a
into
to

not
about
is
today

will
after
it
together

each
again
its
too

about
all
jump
try

how
always
just
two

up
am
keep
under

out
an
kind
up

References

Adams, M.J. *Beginning to Read: Thinking and Learning About Print.* Cambridge: Massachusetts Institute of Technology, 1990.

Allington, R.L. "Fluency: The Neglected Reading Goal." *The Reading Teacher*, 36, 556–561. 1983.

Allington, R.L. "Oral Reading." In D.D. Pearson (ed.), *Handbook of Reading Research.* NY: Longman. 1984.

Anderson, R.C., E.H. Hiebert, J.A. Scott, and I.A.G. Wilkinson. *Becoming a Nation of Readers: The Report of the Commission on Reading.* Champaign, IL: The Center for the Study of Reading and The National Academy of Education. 1985.

Anderson, R.C., P. Wilson, L. Fielding. "Growth in Reading and How Children Spend Their Time Outside of School." *Reading Research Quarterly*, 23, 285–303. 1998.

Anderson , R.C. "The Missing Ingredient: Fluent Oral Reading." *The Elementary School Journal*, 81, 173–177. 1981.

Beck, I., and C. Juel. "The Role of Decoding in Learning to Read." *American Educator.* Summer, 1995.

Biemiller, A. "Relationships Between Oral Reading Rates for Letters, Words, and Simple Text in the Development of Reading Achievement." *Reading Research Quarterly*, Vol. 13. 1970.

Blevins, W. *Phonics from A to Z: A Practical Guide.* NY: Scholastic. 1998.

Blevins, W. *Teaching Phonics and Word Study in the Intermediate Grades.* NY: Scholastic. 2001.

Carreker, S. "Teaching Reading: Accurate Decoding and Fluency" in *Multisensory Teaching of Basic Language Skills.* Edited by J.R. Brisch. Paul Brookes Publishing Co. 1999.

Chall, J.S. *Stages of Reading Development.* McGraw-Hill. 1983.

Chall, J.S. *Stages of Reading Development.* Harcourt Brace & Company. 1996.

Clark, C.H. "Teaching Students About Reading: A Fluency Example." *Reading Horizons*, 35 (3), 251–265. 1995.

Ehri, L.C. "Reconceptualizing the Development of Sight Word Reading and Its Relationship to Recoding" in P. Gough, L. Ehri, and R. Treiman (eds.), *Reading Acquisition.* Hillsdale, NJ: Erlbaum. 1992.

Ehri, L.C. "Phases of Development in Reading Words." *Journal of Research in Reading*, Vol. 18. 1995.

Feldman, K. "Engaged Literacy Learning: Strategies to Maximize Student Participation." Personal Communication. 2001.

Germann, G. "Fluency Norms." Personal Communications. www.edformation.com, 2001.

Hansbrouck, J.E. and G. Tindal. "Curriculum-Based Oral Reading Fluency Norms for Students in Grades 2 Through 5." *Teaching Exceptional Children*, 41–44. 1992.

Harris, T. and R. Hodges (eds.). *The Literacy Dictionary: The Vocabulary of Reading and Writing.* Newark, DE: International Reading Association. 1995.

Hoffman, J.V. "Rethinking the Role of Oral Reading in Basal Instruction." *Elementary School Journal*, 87, 367–373. 1987.

Hoffman J.V. and S. Crone. "The Oral Recitation Lesson: A Research Derived Strategy for Reading in Basal Texts" in J.A. Niles and R.A. Lalik (Eds.) *Issues in Literacy: A Research Perspective, Thirty-fourth Yearbook of the National Reading Conference.* Rochester, NY: National Reading Conference. 1985.

Koskinen, P. and I. Blum. "Paired Repeated Reading: A Classroom Strategy for Developing Fluent Reading." *The Reading Teacher*, 40, 70–75. 1986.

LaBerge, D. and S.J. Samuels. "Toward a Theory of Automatic Information Processing in Reading." *Cognitive Psychology*, 6 (2). 1974.

LaPray, M. and R. Ross. "The Graded Word List: Quick Guage of Reading Ability." *Journal of Reading*, Vol. 12, No. 4. 1969.

Moats, L.C. *Spelling: Development, Disabilities, and Instruction.* Timonium, MD: York Press, Inc. 1995.

Moats, L.C. "The Missing Foundation in Teacher Education." *American Federation of Teachers.* Summer, 1995.

Moats, L.C. "Reading, Spelling, and Writing Disabilities in the Middle Grades" in Wong, B. (Ed.), *Learning About Learning Disabilities*, 2nd Edition, Academic Press. 1998.

Nathan, R.G. and K.E. Stanovich. "The Causes and Consequences of Differences in Reading Fluency." *Theory into Practice*, 30, 176–184 (1991).

Pinnell, G.S., J.J. Pikulski, K.K. Wixson, J.R., Campbell, P.B. Gough, and A.S. Beatty. *Listening to Children Read Aloud.* Office of Educational Research and Improvement, U.S. Department of Education. Washington, D.C. 1995.

Popp, H.M. "Visual Discrimination of Alphabet Letters." *Reading Teacher*, Vol. 17. 1964.

Rasinski, T. "Developing Syntactic Sensitivity in Reading Through Phrase-Cued Texts." *Intervention in School and Clinic*, Vol. 29, No. 3, January 1994.

Rasinski, T. and N. Padak. "Effects of Fluency Development on Urban Second-Graders." Vol. 87, *Journal of Education Research.* 1994.

Richards, M. "Be a Good Detective: Solve the Case of Oral Reading Fluency." *The Reading Teacher*, Vol. 53, 7, pp. 534–539. 2000.

Samuels, S.J. "Decoding and Automaticity: Helping Poor Readers Become Automatic at Word Recognition." *The Reading Teacher.* April, 1988.

Samuels, J. "The Method of Repeated Readings." *The Reading Teacher*, 32, 403–408. 1979.

Samuels, S.J., N. Shermer, and D. Reinking. "Reading Fluency: Techniques for Making Decoding Automatic" in Samuels and Farstrup (Eds.), *What Research Has to Say About Reading Instruction.* (pp. 124–144) Newark, DE: International Reading Association. 1992.

Shefelbine, J. "A Syllabic-Unit Approach to Teaching Decoding of Polysyllabic Words to Fourth- and Sixth-Grade Disabled Readers" in J. Zutell, S. McCormick, M. Connolly, and P. O'Keefe (eds.) *Literacy Theory and Research: Analyses from Multiple Paradigms.* Chicago, IL: National Reading Conference. 1990.

Snow, C.E., M.S. Burns, and P. Griffin. *Preventing Reading Difficulties in Young Children.* Washington, DC: National Academy Press. 1998.

Stanovich, K.E. "Matthew Effects in Reading: Some Consequences of Individual Differences in the Acquisition of Literacy." *Reading Research Quarterly*, Vol. 21. 1986.

Stanovich, K.E. "Romance and Reality." *The Reading Teacher*, Vol. 47, No. 4. December 1993/January 1994.

Taylor, B.M. and L. Nosbush. "Oral Reading for Meaning: A Technique for Improving Word Identification Skills." *The Reading Teacher*, Vol. 37. 1983.